TAKE CHELSEA HOME

Royal Horticultural Society

TAKE CHELSEA HOME

Practical inspiration from
the RHS Chelsea Flower Show

Written by **CHRIS YOUNG**

Foreword by **Alan Titchmarsh**

MITCHELL BEAZLEY

For my wife Nikki, and children Jacob and Isabella, whose
bedtime was always followed by 'Daddy's book'

First published in Great Britain in 2010 by Mitchell Beazley,
an imprint of Octopus Publishing Group Ltd, Endeavour House,
189 Shaftesbury Avenue, London, WC2H 8JY
www.octopusbooks.co.uk

An Hachette UK Company
www.hachette.co.uk

This revised and updated edition published 2013 by Octopus Publishing
Group Ltd in association with The Royal Horticultural Society.

ISBN: 978-1-84533-685-1

A CIP record for this book is available from the British Library.
Colour reproduction by Fine Arts
Printed and bound in China by 1010 Printing International Ltd.

Publisher Alison Starling
RHS Publisher Rae Spencer-Jones
Commissioning Editor Helen Griffin
Editor Joanne Wilson
Copy-editor Joanna Chisholm
Proofreader Lynn Bresler, Kate Fox
Technical Consultant Andrew Wilson
Indexer Diana LeCore
Art Director Pene Parker
Senior Art Editor Juliette Norsworthy
Designer Lizzie Ballantyne
Design Co-ordinator Gary Almond
Picture Research Manager Giulia Hetherington
Senior Production Manager Peter Hunt
Assistant Production Manager Lucy Carter

CONTENTS

Foreword   6
Introduction   8

Chelsea Style   16
Entrances, Paths and Boundaries   26
Planting   50
Outdoor Living   80
Water   104
Materials   130
Sustainability   152
Productive Gardens   174
Lighting   188
Art in the Garden   202

Index of gardens and designers   218
Index   220
Acknowledgements   224

[previous page] A view into the world of the RHS Chelsea Flower Show. Creativity and imagination combine to give endless ideas for the home gardener. Here flat 'slabs' of water are framed by tall tree ferns (*Dicksonia antarctica*).

[left] Bearded iris contrast in shape and texture with rounded heads of *Allium* and dainty, ruffled, pink-cream flowers of *Aquilegia*. Such planting combinations are one of the highlights at Chelsea, with seasonal splendour heralding the arrival of the forthcoming summer.

FOREWORD

You'd think that after attending Chelsea Flower Show for more than forty years a chap might become either blasé or world weary. But neither is the case. Only a cynic could fail to be impressed by the standard of execution, the growing skills and the artistry involved in creating what has been for many years the greatest flower show on earth.

Of course, it's not real. Gardens that appear in three weeks and then disappear overnight cannot possibly be genuine. But that does not mean they are incapable of inspiring you – spurring you on to do better. Like all gardeners the RHS Chelsea Flower Show can make me feel inadequate, but offset against that is its capacity to fire my enthusiasm and renew my passion for gardening.

2013 marks the centenary of the RHS Great Spring Flower Show, and as far as I can see it has never been better. The show gardens created by some of the world's leading designers continue to amaze and court controversy, as well as making us look at things rather differently. Chelsea is the home of haute-culture – the gardening equivalent of the Paris catwalks – where there is no place for the bland and predictable. Its job is to push boundaries, to engender positive emotions, and that it does each year without fail.

But while the gardens may hit the headlines and polarize opinion, no-one could argue that the exhibits of flowers and fruits and vegetables that fill the Great Pavilion are anything other than breathtaking. Whatever the weather

[below left] Chelsea is an international event, with the world's gardening media focused on it, and that includes providing daily television programmes for broadcast.

[bottom left] Caravans are not the first mode of transport to be associated with the show, but on this garden it gives a focal point in a shaded area, while demonstrating that with clever design, even the presence of a mobile home can be beautified.

[below] Nursery displays are the highlight for many visitors, with plants, such as this dazzling display of auriculas, shown off with exacting standards. Such an 'auricula theatre' could be recreated at home.

[below right] Making gardens seem bigger than their actual size is a perennial trick along the Main Avenue each year; views through, mixed planting, and different materials ensure each garden is designed to look great from all angles.

[bottom right] Each year, around 157,000 visitors come to Chelsea, which is always a favourite with the royal family. Her Majesty the Queen, here talking to HRH Prince Charles, is among the regular visitors.

[below] Sculpture is often used on the show gardens – here, the 'bubbly', translucent effect of the sculpture mirrors the circles and holes in the wall behind, keeping a design consistency across the garden.

throws at the growers and exhibitors – and sometimes it has the cruellest of streaks – the gardeners will not let you down. To walk among these displays, which will have come to the banks of the River Thames in London from all over the world, is to witness a gardening legacy.

And that above all, is why Chelsea Flower Show is important: it is a public demonstration of the need to hand on growing skills to future generations. In a world which seems to become more and more reliant on technology, and more and more distanced from nature and the great outdoors, Chelsea Flower Show is a reminder of man's reliance on nature, of the importance of understanding her whims and caprices, and of the wisdom of working with her rather than against her.

This book is a distillation of the show's riches; a memory jogger that will last longer than the week of the show, and a celebration of a hundred years of growing and showing.

I love the Chelsea Flower Show and I admire its ability to celebrate and to nurture both home-grown and international horticultural talent. With any luck it will still be growing strong in a hundred years time – still making those who visit it amazed, outraged, astonished and determined to do their bit to cherish a horticultural heritage that is as old as the hills and every bit as vital.

Alan Titchmarsh MBE VMH DL

INTRODUCTION

Since 1912, the Royal Horticultural Society has hosted the most prestigious flower show in the world. For six days towards the end of May, a small site (4.5 hectares/ 11 acres) in the grounds of the Royal Hospital, London, is transformed into displays of jaw-dropping horticulture. The show welcomes all types of gardeners, and is a cue for them collectively to enjoy one simple pleasure – gardening.

100 YEARS AT THE SHOWGROUND

Exhibiting and display have always been core parts of horticultural history – indeed the desire to impress has gone hand-in-hand with refinement of the craft of growing, the craft of controlling a plant to perform as desired. This, in essence, is at the heart of the 100-year history of the RHS Chelsea Flower Show. It is a show that has mirrored society's tastes, nurserymen's plants and designer's desires, but it has always believed in showing the very best in horticulture.

The Royal Horticultural Society has a long history dating from 1804, with display an essential part of its, and horticulture's, development. Founded under the title The Horticultural Society of London, by Sir Joseph Banks and John Wedgwood, its aim was to collect plant information and encourage the improvement of horticultural practice. Over the following 200 years, it has changed from a tight-knit horticultural society of interested parties, to a organization today that has nearly 400,000 members, and undertakes everything from school gardening to horticultural science.

And shows have always had a key part of RHS life. Their prototypes began in the late 1820s, with a series of floral fetes held at the Duke of Devonshire's estate in Chiswick, London. The 1850s saw a period of financial crisis, due to falling proceeds from the gardens and membership. Prince Albert, the Society's then President, revived its fortunes by arranging a new charter in 1861, resulting in the name, The Royal Horticultural Society. A new garden in Kensington was also secured (which remained its headquarters until 1888) which hosted the first Great Spring Show in 1862. Some 26 years later, in 1888, the Great Spring Show moved to the gardens of the Inner Temple (one of the four Inns of Court in London) where it survived until 1911.

It was at this time that the Chelsea Flower Show we know today started its gestation. When the last Temple Show finished, the following year (1912) the Great Spring Show was cancelled in order that the RHS could work with other organisations on staging the Royal International Horticultural Exhibition. And the

[above right] Staging a display at the show has always depended on plentiful imagination and hard graft – as these gardeners tending a rock garden display in 1924 well prove. Add colour to the picture (and change the clothes) and there would be little difference from the work that goes on today.

[below right] One of the consistent things about Chelsea is the interest from the public. Fashions may have changed (this picture was taken in 1936), but the crowd's enjoyment endures.

A Chelsea timeline

Some key dates and events in Chelsea's history:

- **1913**
  The original 'Great Spring Show' (now called the RHS Chelsea Flower Show) moves to the Chelsea Hospital, a three day event (it only became a five-day event (Tues–Sat) in 2005)

- **1917–18**
  Chelsea Flower Show cancelled for the duration of the First World War

- **1926**
  Chelsea Flower Show held a week later than scheduled because of the General Strike

- **1930**
  The multiplicity of tents is reduced into a single four-span marquee for a while

- **1940–46**
  Chelsea Flower Show cancelled for the duration of the Second World War

- **1948**
  A corner of one of the marquees is devoted to flower arranging for the first time

- **1949**
  Show extended to four days (Tues–Fri)

  The two marquees are replaced by a single gigantic marquee, which featured in the Guinness Book of Records as the world's largest

- **1951**
  This is also the year of the Festival of Britain, and Chelsea is themed as a festival show; RHS Garden Wisley gardeners stage a massive Himalayan display, the largest staged under the marquee until that time

- **1956**
  A separate tent for flower arranging is introduced this year

- **1968**
  For the first time, no commercial firm applies to stage a rock garden; the gardeners from RHS Garden Wisley in Surrey step in and stage one

[above] Connections with the Royal Family have long been a mainstay for the Chelsea Flower Show. Here, in 1934, Queen Mary (the Queen's grandmother) is followed by her entourage while looking at a pond.

[below] A view into an immaculately created Japanese-inspired garden at Chelsea in 1936.

[above] In 1927, a young Princess Mary (King George V and Queen Mary's daughter) inspects the bountiful flowerheads of hydrangeas.

[below] The 3rd Lord Aberconway (who owned Bodnant Garden, North Wales) was RHS President for 23 years, from 1961 to 1984. Here he is guiding Queen Elizabeth II around the show, as is the honour for RHS Presidents.

CHELSEA SHOW 1913

[left] RHS staff may have changed their appearance since this photograph in 1913, but the skill and passion to make sure this show is a success for all visitors remains true today.

location of this exhibition? In the grounds of the Chelsea Hospital, the retirement home and nursing home for British soldiers (which was founded by King Charles II in 1682).

The Great Spring Show, as some still nostalgically refer to it, moved to the Chelsea Hospital and started life, as a three-day event, from 1913. The past 100 years has seen great change: the original massing of tents for plant display has been replaced by today's single span construction; the show length has changed from three to five days; key areas such as 'Rock Bank' remain but no longer are home to alpine-related display gardens; show garden budgets continue to expand and create bigger spectacle (in 2011 Diarmuid Gavin introduced a crane as part of his 'sky' garden); and the relationship with media (and television in particular) remains essential to its ability to inform millions across the world.

Like all good British traditions, Chelsea is an extravagance, a show spectacle that some may feel is unnecessary or others may marvel at. Some of it may be unachievable, but it is never short on excellence, drama or inspiration. It is, in short, still the best show on earth if you enjoy gardening. And may that continue for another 100 years.

[below] The photographs may be more colourful, but the desire to bring delightful gardens and spectacular plants to a small corner of London each May has continued for 100 years – and, we hope, for many more to come.

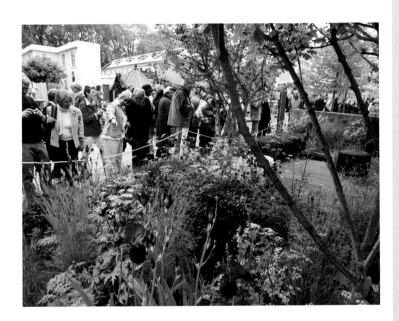

- **1971**
  Chelsea weather: widespread flooding of the show site
- **1979**
  Crowding is so severe that the turnstiles are temporarily closed
- **1980**
  The BBC funds a garden by the Beaminster District Gardens and Allotment Society, the first to be created by a local horticultural society, prompting press fears about the impact of sponsorship
- **1988**
  Ceiling imposed on the number of tickets issued (limit of 40,000 per day), and RHS members charged for Chelsea tickets for the first time
- **1989**
  First Chelsea Gala held on the Monday evening
- **1997**
  Christopher Bradley-Hole gets best in show for 'The Latin Garden'
- **1999**
  Landscape designer Michael Balston's 'Reflections' garden becomes the first Chelsea garden to be re-erected as a model garden at RHS Garden Wisley after the show
- **2000**
  New pavilion erected to replace the old marquee
- **2009**
  BBC television presenter James May's plasticine garden
- **2012**
  This sees the tallest show garden, in the form of Diarmuid Gavin's 24 metre pyramidal tower

Compiled by Brent Elliott, RHS Historian

Chelsea garden selection... and judging

Most show gardens have a lead-in period of two to three years, but applications for the Chelsea Flower Show have to be received by the RHS during July of the previous year. These include perspective views, planting lists, construction details and the 'client's brief', showing the background of the design and proposed theme.

The RHS annually appoints a seven-strong selection panel representing landscape and garden designers, horticulturalists and members of the media, to decide which of these gardens will be seen at the following year's Chelsea. Their role is to ensure that all aspects of the garden have been considered – there is no attempt at redesign. The final cut is made in September and the gardens are allocated space during November. From then on is a frantic time for the designer, contractor, grower and sponsor.

The judging panels normally comprise seven panel members including designers, contractors and growers, and three garden assessors, who meet on the Sunday before Chelsea opens to the public; they scrutinise the detail of each garden with an updated client brief. Marks are awarded from the marking sheet which provide a maximum of 10% for brief and purpose, 20% for overall design, 30% for planting, 20% for construction, and 20% for overall impression. Following discussion, voting takes place and a final medal recommendation is made.

The recommendations of the judging panels go to a moderation meeting which is attended by all of the assessors, judges and by three moderators who ensure that the results are fair and consistent, not only across Chelsea Flower Show but across all RHS shows. Each recommendation is considered in turn, and moderators can challenge or discuss any aspect of the judging panel's views.

Votes take place for any garden on which there is contention, and finally the awards are agreed. There is a press embargo on the release of the garden awards until 7am on Tuesday.

CHELSEA TODAY

The RHS Chelsea Flower Show is where horticultural ideas get aired, messages publicised and materials trialled. It gets people's minds racing, showing the infinite ideas you can take home for your garden. In short, it offers something for almost every taste in gardening. The show brings together designers, nurserymen, enthusiastic amateurs and educational establishments, all of whom give their take on horticulture. Yet it is also the visitors who help make the show special. Stand in among the throng and you get to hear heartfelt honest opinions – you soon learn if a display is popular or not. Such wide-ranging diversity of opinion makes Chelsea stimulating, exciting and, for exhibitors, somewhat daunting.

Horticultural variety is displayed in three main ways at the show: the Great Pavilion, the show gardens and the trade stands. The pavilion hosts the splendour and spectacle of horticulture at its best: rows of flowers in ultimate bloom; planting scenes showing off a nursery's deft touch; and sublime floral displays. The show gardens are the domain of the designers, demonstrating garden-making

[below] Every part of a Chelsea garden must be meticulously planned, designed, built and cared for. The final tweaking continues right until the judges arrive for the last time, before casting their votes.

[above] Many of the most popular gardens at the show bring a substantial quality of design and detail to the viewing public. By mixing many well known, and some rarer, plants in with high-quality hard landscaping, inspiring and truly desirable gardens are created.

[below] One of the key challenges for a designer at the show is to challenge themselves with new ideas or solutions. Whether introducing new materials, or selecting bold bright colours, every design is considered and constantly refined until the very last minute.

at its best. Finally, the trade stands, dotted throughout the showground, allow the horticultural industry to showcase its range of products – from sit-on tractors to greenhouses.

The planning, co-ordination and energy needed to pull off any kind of display are huge. So why do people, whether amateur plant collector or renowned designer, do it? In short, it is the thrill of possibly receiving an RHS gold medal, and being able to talk with like-minded professionals and amateur gardeners.

To stage a Chelsea show garden can be a considerable cost, and most designers rely on a sponsor (see panel, p15) to help in part or fully with the cost; contractors, material suppliers and associated supporters are also involved. A good Chelsea show garden should inform, inspire and suggest possibilities, and most of the 157,000 visitors normally find at least one aspect of a garden from which they can draw ideas. There are three main types of garden: the 'Artisan' gardens which demonstrate what can be achieved in a small plot, and with the beautiful woodland of Ranelagh Gardens as a backdrop; larger 'Show' ones can be up to 10 x 22m (30 x 70ft) and normally attract the big-name designers; and, introduced in 2012 for the first time, a new category called 'Fresh', which aim to encourage innovation and the creative use of materials. Together, the three types of gardens offer something for all tastes and interests.

Even though they mirror the scale of many private gardens, there is an important issue to remember. Chelsea show gardens are stage sets, created for their ability to wow and excite, in which the walls may not be made as they would be in a 'real' garden; the planting combinations may not be sustainable for long-term growth; some plants may have been forced on or kept back to ensure they flower at the end of May; and the longevity of materials chosen may not survive a season in a 'normal' garden. Despite this, after Chelsea has ended, show gardens are often relocated – maybe to a school, housing association or private client.

In some ways, Chelsea feels like a show split in two. The first part involves the tension of the build-up, finishing the gardens and the judging on the Monday morning. Then, that afternoon, the show relaxes slightly during the visit by the royal family, affording nurserymen, designers and trade representatives time to meet the royals. On the Tuesday, the awards are announced first thing, and the public enjoy the show until the end, on the Saturday afternoon. Then everyone, tired but exhilarated, departs – with bundles of flowers in the arms of the fortunate few. Yet, for all the pomp, ceremony, hard work and money on display, the common interest of gardening, and really wanting to make a garden better, perhaps underline why the RHS Chelsea Flower Show continues to be such an enduring success.

[left] There are some sublime touches of beautiful design with refined horticulture at the show – here, *Rosa* 'Reine des Violettes' grows over wicker baskets to give a mounded and colourful addition to the planting.

[below] The television coverage of Chelsea is an essential part of the media's work, and in 2012 presenter Joe Swift took time off from presenting the main programme to design this garden. Pleasingly, his garden was awarded gold; not bad for a first-time entrant to the show.

[right] Bold visual displays are also part of this show's magic. When Diarmuid Gavin asked for the Chelsea pensioners, suitably attired in their scarlet coats and tricorne hats, to climb onto his seven-storey 'pyramid' garden, it was a moving tribute to the people who live on the site of this annual show.

Matching idealism with reality

With the average cost of a Chelsea show garden being £150,000, it is essential to secure a sponsor, yet for a designer this search can be harder than designing the garden itself. He or she can spend months seeking money, or else they can sit back and hope a sponsor comes along. Sometimes the designer's idea is pitched to a potential sponsor, while at other times a designer secures a sponsor first and then works out the design.

'In an ideal world the green light from the sponsor comes in June,' said Andy Sturgeon, winner of many gold-medal show gardens at Chelsea. Once the design has been agreed, the detail of the garden gets worked up and is submitted to the RHS selection panel for approval (see panel, p12). Until acceptance is received (by autumn), designers have something of a dilemma. In the interim they have to go out and buy all the plants without even knowing if they will be awarded a plot.

From February, press releases and PR activity for RHS Chelsea Flower Show ramp up excitement levels and, according to Sturgeon, 'help put the pressure on you as the designer. As you start to visit your plants, you really get a feel for how the design might end up looking.'

The contractor starts on site in early May: trees go in during the first week, with all the construction (ideally) being finished after 12 days, leaving a week to complete the planting. However, most gardens aren't finished until Sunday afternoon – or even later, aided by van headlights. That day and the Monday can be a really stressful time for each designer, while assessing and judging are taking place.

Monday is press day, too, when each designer needs to give interviews to the media. 'That night you try to catch up on your sleep but you can't until the medals are put out on the winning gardens. This is done early on Tuesday morning, and there are always tears – either of joy or sadness,' reflected Sturgeon.

CHELSEA STYLE

Over the years the RHS Chelsea Flower Show has helped to endear us to many garden styles. From cottage gardens to formal areas, wildflower meadows to contemporary spaces, the gardens have used an array of styles, materials and ideas. Yet, increasingly, few gardens fit easily into a pigeonhole of a defined 'style', because designers have blended elements of different genres into their exhibits.

[left] An understanding of spatial division is at the heart of great contemporary design, which here has a restrained, interesting and modern feel.

[below] In their romantic gardens, Chelsea designers often include escapist elements such as this boat amid the billowing planting, to entice visitors to revel in their dreams.

Some of these mixed-style gardens are themed and relay a message, while other types of show garden might be artistic or conceptual. Either way, they may use formal or romantic elements (for example), but they can't be defined as a 'formal' or 'romantic' garden *per se*. And it is often this amalgamation of styles that makes the RHS Chelsea Flower Show so utterly absorbing, as visitors question what they see and think differently about a preconceived notion of a particular garden style.

ROMANTIC

Possibly one of the most popular garden styles seen at Chelsea, successful romantic gardens should exude masses of atmosphere, include an abundance of planting and evoke a feeling of femininity and sumptuousness. This can be a big challenge for garden designers, especially as so much depends on successful planting – roses, bearded iris, flowering shrubs and colour-coordinated summer bedding are just a few prerequisites. The end result should be an attractively planted garden, supported by a well-positioned sculpture, seating or artefact. Views should be considered so that a heightened level of enjoyment and focus can be achieved. Small areas for sitting as well as intimate spaces and hidden gems add excitement. You too can create a romantic garden relatively easily, as long as the romantic side of you is allowed unrestricted scope.

MINIMALIST

This style can often be the most divisive at Chelsea for it polarises popular opinion. Supporters respect the clean lines, the unfussy nature of the planting, the thoughtful selection of materials, the fact that such gardens can be conveniently 'low maintenance' and the consideration given to every element in such gardens. By contrast, detractors state that this contemporary style is soulless, impersonal and, because it often uses a minimal material palette, uninteresting. Whatever your take, there is no doubting the thought that designers give to create such impressive spaces. Colour can be vivid, bold and almost garish; at other times the range may be cooler, calmer and restrained. Modern contemporary gardens are particularly popular in urban environments, where gardens may not need to respond to the vernacular of local buildings and landscape as they might in the countryside. Such a style, however, isn't as easy to achieve as it looks. In really good examples, the way that people will use the space is understood, the spatial balance of the garden is exemplary, and its texture and tones of materials are well matched. If you can interpret such design principles successfully, then the end result could be hugely exciting.

MEDITERRANEAN

Simple colours, bright flowers and bold foliage, coloured rendered walls, succulent plants or cacti, outdoor furniture and shade-giving trees or screens epitomise this style. It is based on growing plants on often poor soil, with limited water, in warm dry heat. Although this is possibly the easiest garden style to conjure up in your mind – most people think of holidays past – it is actually quite difficult in

reality to achieve a convincing Mediterranean-styled garden without it looking tokenistic or inappropriate, especially if your area is prone to grey clouds and high moisture levels. Remember that terracotta is a given (whether tiled floors or containers), as is a simplicity in planting choice. But perhaps, most importantly, Mediterranean-style gardens yearn to be used and enjoyed.

ARABIC

Stone walls, coloured tiles, simplified water features, fruit trees, vertical accents of conifers or cypresses, palm trees and symbolic meanings can often be found in an Arabic garden. There is something endlessly sophisticated about the way designers interpret this style of garden at Chelsea. Restrained use of materials is important, but it is how those pieces are put together that really counts. Symmetry and geometry are essential, helping to create an air of order and gracefulness. An Arabic garden has a calm ambience that slows down the visitor and allows them fully to appreciate the scene as well as the materials and atmosphere therein. Well-conceived Arabic gardens may be difficult to create convincingly in your garden, so consider making a 'garden room' or just a part of your outdoor space based on this theme.

[above] Classically inspired schemes, here mixing contemporary detailing with formal lines, can be introduced successfully – in both large and small spaces.

[left] Hinting at the warm climes of the Mediterranean, orange-flowered *Geum* 'Totally Tangerine' combines with the spiky leaves of an *Aloe*. The result is a warm yet architectural feel.

[right] The colours and textures in this restful Persian-inspired garden encourage the visitor to pause and reflect in an otherwise busy world.

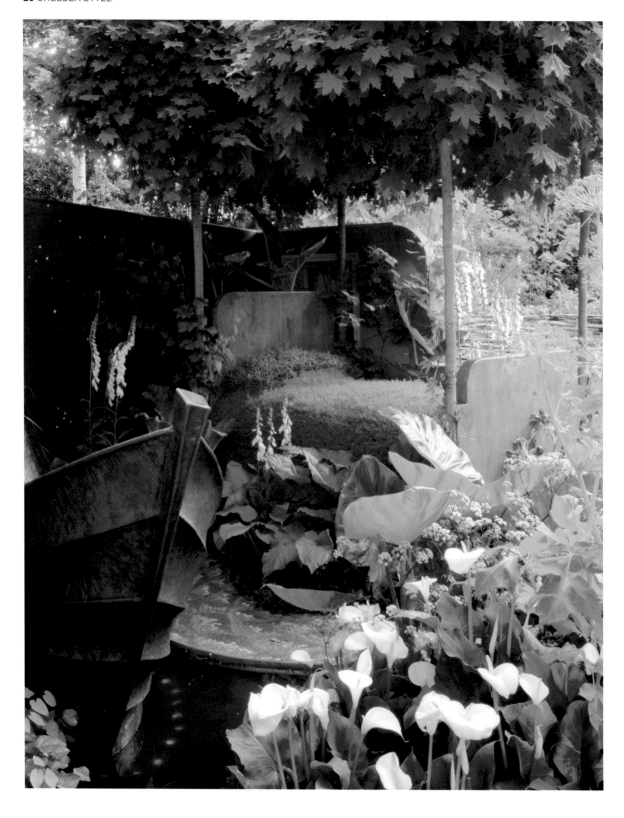

CLASSIC

There is a timelessness to classic gardens that is often interpreted by other styles, fashions and people. Influences from France, English country estates and grand designs on a large-scale landscape are primary drivers. Sometimes a modern interpretation can be overlain on a classic garden, yet the tone still tends to be formal and reserved. The visitor is expected to experience a classic garden by walking through it, maybe sitting in predetermined seating areas, and having an 'arm's length' relationship with the planting. When done well, such a garden exudes an air of good quality and high class that few other garden styles can emulate. Yet these gardens are not cold or lifeless. Moreover, their structure, composition and feeling are quite easy for you to recreate in your garden.

TELLING A TALE

Chelsea designers often use their opportunity at the show to impart a message or relate a story. The end result can often be fun and good natured; at other times it can be subtle and subliminal. Some designers take their inspiration from literature or revered personalities: for example, Swedish landscape architect Ulf Nordfjell's sublime garden in 2007 paid tribute to the work of botanist, scientist and explorer Carl Linnaeus, celebrating his tercentenary and referencing the breadth of work he undertook. Others provide their interpretation of a particular topic or else recreate elements from a particular place: one garden, entitled 'I dream, I seek my garden' by Chinese garden designer Shao Fan in 2008, brought a new take on Chinese art forms, recreating a scholar's garden full of contemporary and traditional influences. Referencing an event, person or place through the medium of a show garden not only gives a firm basis for a design, but it can also be a hugely successful way of engaging with the show's visitors. In your own garden, be careful how the meaning of your story is imparted; subtlety is often safer than an overt link to a place, person or historical event, which can end up as a cliché.

WILDLIFE

Some designers use the RHS Chelsea Flower Show to emphasise the importance of wildlife in the garden and provide an understanding of how wildlife fits into the wider environment. This is often done by imparting a specific message – the reasons to garden organically or to attract certain types of wildlife, for example – or by showing that wildlife and gardening can be in harmony. Research is confirming that a balanced mix of plant types and areas of hard landscaping can offer a great habitat for wildlife. Fortunately, a diverse range of garden styles can offer attractive homes for a wide range of creatures, so overall design doesn't have to be compromised. By looking closely at the gardens on display at the show, you will

[left] A bed and a boat hint at the basis of a story, leaving the viewer to interpret the other elements of the tableau.

[below] Increasingly, both homeowners and gardeners are realising the vital relationship between garden and wildlife. Here, some intriguing vertical 'insect hotels' offer refuge for all types of fauna, which are just a short hop or flight from the nearest flowers.

discover how wildlife and gardening integrate when sharing the same area. Your garden can relate to this approach, as long as it has varied garden elements.

FORMAL

There is an ingrained sense of grandeur, balance and structure in formal gardens. For a vast number of people this is fundamentally appealing, yet for others such gardens can be too rigid and unemotional. Maybe the attraction of formal gardens relates to the gardener's dominance over the natural landscape, or possibly it is because there is a natural aesthetic that balances scale and proportion, which sits comfortably with a viewer's eye. Yet again, it might be because formal rules can influence a range of other styles: modern or contemporary gardens have embraced formality; Mediterranean and Arabic gardens include formal elements; and even wildflower meadows can be created within a formal grid. You can easily introduce an element of formality into your garden, by including rounded box balls, tightly clipped hedging and restrained planting. The only challenge most gardeners face, however, is to maintain the self-discipline that is needed to keep within formal design principles.

MAGICAL AND MAD

Sometimes designers just want to throw away the shackles of tradition. Maybe they have been inspired by a painting or song, or perhaps they have had a great idea but never until RHS Chelsea Flower Show had the opportunity to build on it. Either way, these types of show gardens make for great effect.

One of the tenets is that there are no rules – the gardens are unpredictable, fun, quirky, fascinating, challenging, uncomfortable or just plain weird. Take, for example, the evocative dreaming 'girl', lying in 'The 4head garden of dreams' (designed by Marney Hall and Heather Yarrow). The living sculpture was created by Sue and Peter Hill, who used plants and other materials to create a mystical and otherworldly feel, transporting visitors into a relaxing and peaceful place. For the visiting public at Chelsea there may be confusion about the garden's intention, but sometimes that would be to miss the point: 'magical and mad' gardens celebrate diversity and are dedicated to the pursuit of creative energy. Some of these gardens may be deemed 'fun' or 'silly', but that would be to belittle the skill of making them. Trying out a style in your garden is a considerable challenge, and one that can be achieved only with the right technical skill.

[right] Making the formal informal, designer Tom Stuart-Smith has created an exquisitely proportioned space that could be at home in any garden. The simple, rectangular pool references classical design elements, yet the undulating, cloud-like box hedging on the right makes the straight lines of the pool more informal. Add to that the loose and almost hedge-row inspired planting in the foreground, and this is a cleverly considered 'formal garden'. The open-sided garden 'room' at the end of the pool is a beautiful focal point and yet has contemporary architecture making it feel right up-to-date.

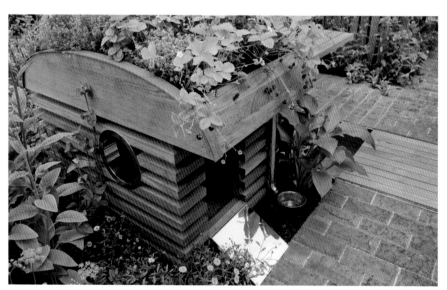

[left] There are no details too small or too bizarre for Chelsea designers: here, a modern take on a dog kennel has been included, with exacting design detail. Note the productive nature of the roof, with strawberries and herbs overhanging, as well as the steel downpipe that feeds into the dog's water bowl. Making use of all surfaces and spaces of a garden not only maximises productivity, but as here, can bring a smile to the face of anyone who comes across it – whether man or beast.

The long, straight lines here result from a clever use of texture and colour. Precision construction adds to the air of quality and skill. The tiered hedging, at the back of the garden, is a modern look and can be achieved with yew, box or rosemary.

The Laurent-Perrier Garden, Luciano Giubbilei, 2009

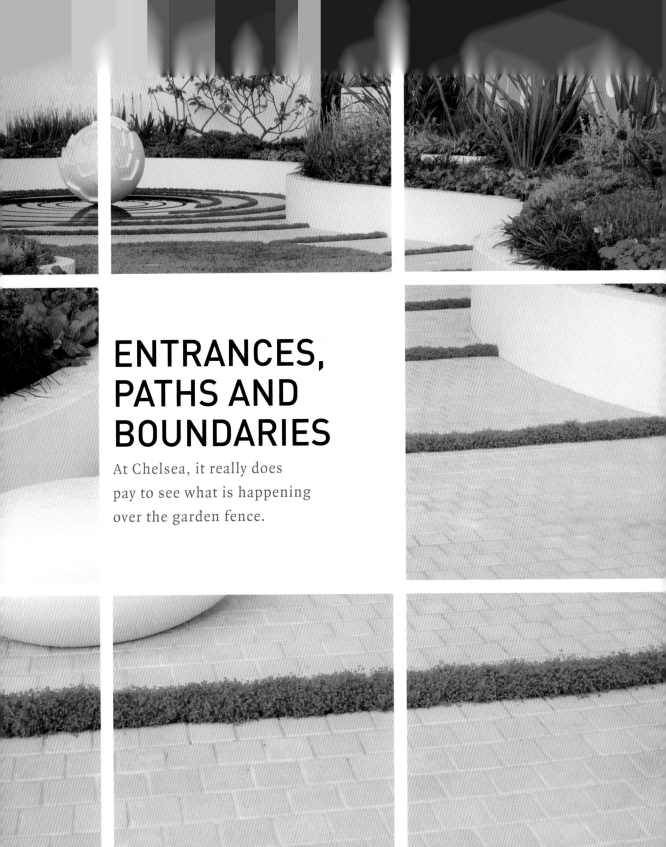

ENTRANCES, PATHS AND BOUNDARIES

At Chelsea, it really does
pay to see what is happening
over the garden fence.

The relationship between elements such as steps, planting, walls, furniture, water features, paving, fencing and buildings is at the heart of good design. Many of the materials used at Chelsea are available to gardeners, and designers such as Sarah Eberle (see case study, p100) and Diarmuid Gavin (see p198) have worked with manufacturers on new products.

Consider first how the entrance, paving, walls, fences and steps are laid out, and what they are made of. For some, their success may lie in their use of materials that blend into the background, acting as a supporting role to plants; in other places, it may be the walls or paths that are the defining features themselves, setting the style of the garden.

Entrances can range from gates, doors and arches to trelliswork and screens. Such devices are not that often included at Chelsea, because these gardens aren't necessarily big enough to allow – or require – the space to be divided by different entrances. However, some show gardens do start off with a bold entrance (such as an archway or moon gate; see Jinny Blom case study, p46) to frame a view and really focus the attention of the visitor.

As you step into a garden, it is perhaps the material on the ground that is the next priority. From small square setts to reclaimed old York stone, from timber decking to recycled rubber mats, paving choices can be as varied as the imagination. But perhaps the main lesson from Chelsea is that the fewer materials competing for your attention the better: with paving, less really is more. This doesn't mean that having, for example, decking butting up to clay bricks laid on edge won't 'work'; it is just that thought must be given as to how these materials will look together, how they age, their construction needs and practical issues of usability. There are no rights or wrongs, but care must be paid.

Often forgotten is the role that fences or walls play. Whether it be their colours, materials or shape, how you demarcate your boundary should be given serious thought, especially when you consider just how much of a boundary you are likely to see in your day-to-day life. Walls are aesthetically appealing, but brick or stone can be hugely expensive and may need planning approval. Yet, if you are planning on staying in your house for some years, and aware that you will be seeing a lot of your boundary, then money on a wall may be well spent. The way a wall ages adds a sense of maturity to a plot. It creates a microclimate of its that is often underestimated. Fencing, too, is effective, and Chelsea designers, as ever, introduce new techniques and approaches to this type of boundary material.

1 Industrial mesh has been used as a walkway, flanked by reflective kickboards and shade-tolerant planting, resulting in a modern, clean and effective combination of materials (see case study, p102-3).

2 Small gardens feel bigger when boundaries are hidden from view. Ribbons of planting continue from the ground up onto the walls, as do the rounded concrete structures. Their colour, shapes and texture give little clue as to where the garden stops and starts.

3 The relationship of materials – 'hard' (physical entities) and 'soft' (planting) – is crucial to good design. This deck is made from Ipe timber boards set on edge, with 15mm (½in) gaps between. The gaps allow planting to soften the edges and grow between the boards.

4 Bespoke iron railings add interest and detail to this brick wall. With the dense hedge beyond, it is a subtle way of keeping intruders out of the garden.

When Chelsea designers do divide space, the end result is that a garden often feels bigger. How have they done this? Mainly by separating areas of the garden with hedging (such as box or hornbeam, often tightly clipped) or with man-made screens such as trelliswork, small walls, vertical posts, Perspex screens and glass.

One of the consistent themes running through the designs at Chelsea is that of innovation. Whether it be the designer's overall plan bringing new ideas together, or his or her collaborations with other artisans or engineers, each year sees a new or adapted technique brought to the fore. For some years, it was plastics and Perspex – whether as water sculptures, seating, tables, screens or containers. Other years have seen glass, perforated metal or rusting steel used to great effect. Recycled CDs, crushed glass mulch, recycled plastics or by-products of the timber industry have also been adopted, for planters, paths, walls or surface decoration.

The end result has been radical uses and new applications of materials, making the show gardens exciting and challenging. At Chelsea, it really does pay to see what is happening over the garden fence.

Steps with visual interest

Dealing with differences in height is a challenge – whether it be a few centimetres over a small distance or gradient changes that require substantial earth moving. The principle for either is the same, though. The gardener is required to move soil or rock into level areas so that access is made bearable by users of that space.

While steps are a practical and physical necessity for most, they also add much in terms of visual interest; in addition, their design contribution should not be underestimated. From contemporary clean lines to rustic charm, from recycled to manufactured materials, steps can be created from an almost endless list of possibilities. Technical concerns, such as structural rigidity and comfort of travel, must also be considered, as well as the safety of steps, especially taking into account how different materials respond in different weather conditions.

1

2

EXPERT TIP

Adam Frost
How to design your steps

❝ Altering levels in a garden adds interest and movement and is often necessary. Such a change can be enhanced by using steps that are more generously sized than maybe they need to be in order to make an area look wider than it actually is. This works well when approaching a door or gate. At the other end of the spectrum, keeping steps shallow and narrow can add to a sense of tension when entering a space.

Key points to think about when you are creating steps:

- When choosing the materials for your steps, take your lead from the other surfaces in the garden. Timber steps tend to be an easy and cheap way of dealing with level changes, while steps made from hard materials will require concrete foundations. Also bear safety in mind, especially for your choice of tread material (the actual step itself). Non-slip materials may be appropriate in some circumstances.
- A visual warning of the change in level is needed, possibly by laying a different material at the top of the flight.
- People should be able to travel up and down steps comfortably. To achieve this, the general rule is to have

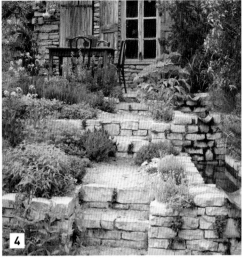

STEPPING UP TO THE MARK

Steps can be simple or complicated, made in a range of design styles, for short- or long-term use.

1 Cut logs have been set on end to give a rustic and 'eco' feel to this subtly sweeping stepped path. The use of varying size, length and girth adds interest, but can give a relatively uneven walking surface.

2 Beige-white diamond-sawn limestone slabs give a clean contemporary feel, accentuated by the dark shadows underneath. The soft grasses and other perennials reinforce the linear nature of the stone.

3 Clever effects have been achieved with a variety of materials. The mesh-topped gabions (filled with rock) give an industrial feel and contrast with the more 'domestic', smooth walls and cobbled pathway.

4 A rustic feel to this Provence-style garden has been achieved with the consistent use of stonework for steps, paving and walling. The steps are in line with the building's window, allowing the user a line of sight to the property.

the rise of the step around 15cm (6in) high and the tread should never be smaller than 30cm (12in) across.

- Steps need to be inviting, and wider flights can be more welcoming than narrow ones.
- Changes of direction such as a curve or sweep in the flight of steps gives the user several vistas onto the garden as they proceed up or down.
- Lit steps can look beautiful and add an enchanting air of elegance, as well as safety at night-time.
- For a steep flight of steps, it may be necessary to create a grab rail (this could either a freestanding or wall mounted design) for people to use as a support. ⟩

Achieving the correct rise and tread is crucial to ensure a flight of steps is comfortable and user-friendly.

Walls for vertical wonder

At first sight, the physical presence of a wall might seem an immovable oppressive feature. Yet, with imagination and a clear understanding of your plot, a wall can offer an array of possibilities: it can be painted or faced to change its colour or texture; it can be planted against or on, bringing vegetation to a vertical plane; it can act as a microclimate allowing for a wide range of plants to be grown; and it could be created into something sculptural and visually exciting. Practical concerns, of course, must be thought through. What direction is the wall facing? Will it be mainly sunny or shaded? How high is it? Is there any planting area at its base? Who owns the structure? Will any changes affect the rigidity of it? But once these serious questions are answered, a wall need not be a blight on the gardener's landscape – with creativity and flair it could become a great gardening asset.

SMOOTH WALLS AND CLEAN FINISHES

With a little bit of imagination and some appropriate design, walls can be transformed into stylish and contemporary features.

1 By dividing the face of this large wall into sections filled with climbing ivy (*Hedera*), this living backdrop exudes permanence and solidity.

2 Rammed earth walls display a stunning patina of colour and pattern. The textured finish is a great backdrop to the planting in front.

3 Moss tracks have been inset into a smooth finish render, but this example would need irrigation to prevent the moss drying out on a vertical structure. Moss must never be collected from wild areas.

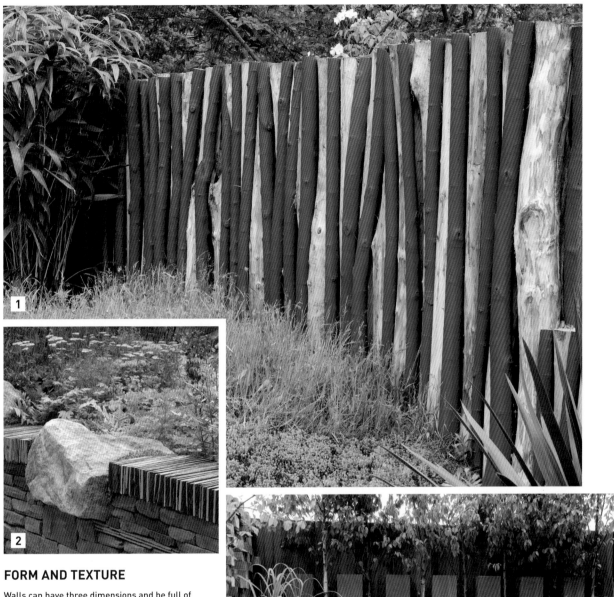

FORM AND TEXTURE

Walls can have three dimensions and be full of pace, movement and creativity.

1 A row of painted and natural, stripped-bark trunks forms a 'moving' wall. Because of this bold design statement, the surrounding planting needs to complement, not compete, with the wall.

2 Contrasting materials add interest to small spaces. Here a sandstone boulder juts out from the dry-stone wall below, in line with slates turned on edge.

3 Rusting steelwork, cut and carved into a chequerboard shape, not only conceals the far wall but also makes a huge statement. This structure houses birch (*Betula*) trees behind it – the white-grey of the trunks can be glimpsed through the open squares. Over time, the steel will darken.

The size of this garden has been accentuated by use of strong horizontals (white-painted walls) and verticals (white bark on the birch trees). This technique, coupled with overflowing planting, helps reduce the dominance of paths and walls.

The Savills Garden, Marcus Barnett and Philip Nixon, 2006

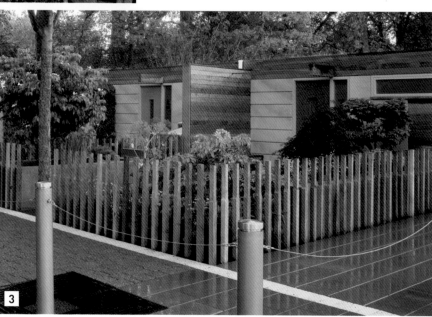

LOW-KEY FENCING

Fences are most commonly made of wood or metal. Their role can be subtle or obvious, and should always reflect the surrounding aesthetic.

1 Reused pieces of timber have been nailed together to create an informal but highly successful spatial divide, allowing roses to grow and entwine through them.

2 Hooped-ring iron railings may have a municipal feel to them, but here have been 'softened' by the stunning display of red poppies and other wild flowers. The formality of the railings makes for an interesting contrast with the informality of the annual flowers.

3 In urban areas, especially in terraced housing, front garden spaces play a significant role in 'greening' the urban environment. Here, contemporary tapered-end, wooden posts show where public space ends and private garden begins. The gaps between each post 'soften' the look of the fencing and allow plants to grow through them.

Defining space: fences and screens

Whether it is your boundary or an internal area, how you divide up a garden is an essential part of design. The use of fencing for such divisions is a feature for many outdoor plots, and there are a range of sizes, colours and materials to select. Their style, strength and longevity need consideration, whether it be of formal, traditional iron railings or more informal, rustic wooden examples. Practical concerns of how the fence is secured into the ground are also important, as are whether the fence abuts a public space and what could grow on or against it.

Screens, on the other hand, tend to subdivide space within an existing garden area – to create pockets of interest, provide backdrops and focal points, or to suggest direction of travel. Their role and creation must be well thought through – it is never easy to move a physical structure.

STYLISH SCREENS FOR PERSONAL SPACE

Screens – whether large or small, man-made or natural, coloured or textured – can actually help make a garden feel bigger.

1 Semi-transparent screens give an illusion of space and depth to a garden – painted black they allow light-and-shadow play. The circular cut-out adds a sense of adventure to the whole experience.

2 This white screen not only curves round a corner but also folds over at the top a little, triggering a sense of enclosure and safety for those sitting on the glass deck below.

3 Toughened glass is increasingly used in gardens to divide space while permitting light and views through.

Stylish and useful paths

How you traverse your space and how it looks are fundamental factors in creating paths or walking surfaces through a garden. Paths can meander at a gentle pace, encouraging you to absorb the surroundings, or they can aid quick and easy movement to a specific area. Decisions should focus on: what the role of the path is to be; how long it is expected to last; what level of maintenance is required; and what types of materials could be used. Consider also the physical presence of the path, and how its inclusion may divide or harmonise your space. If your garden includes a dominant path as a central design feature, then its materials and construction must be of a very high quality – it will come under scrutiny from all quarters. Natural stone is a popular choice of path material, while other hard landscaping materials can sometimes provide much needed colour.

1

MATERIAL INTEREST

Curving paths are popular in less formal design schemes, softening the overall route through a garden.

1 This raised and curved walkway consists of wooden decking and circular concrete 'landing pads'.

2 The straight lines of this brick-edged path have been softened by the inclusion of camomile, which draws the eye along and up to the rest of the garden's borders. The paving slabs inset into the plants mean the path remains useful.

3 The rough nature of these bricks adds a texture and colour variation to the path. By including such a path in a home scheme, visual interest is maintained throughout the year, as well as providing a complementary backdrop to the planting.

2

3

GETTING STRAIGHT TO THE POINT

Simple linear paving is often attributed to modern designs, but can be used for any style garden. The result is often a pared-down approach, allowing the materials themselves or associated planting to shine.

1 Diamond-sawn sandstone slabs divide the water's edge from the planting. The buff-beige colour acts as a cool and subtle tone; the fact that the slabs have been precision cut adds a contemporary feel.

2 This long view through dense, low-growing planting shows how well a path can be confined to a supporting role. By allowing the plants to overspill the edges, an informal effect is created and the visitor is encouraged to carry on and reach the end of the path.

3 A cuboid theme linking the wood block seat and square stone blocks beneath is complemented by use of the same stone for the longer slabs flanking the water feature. This design principle brings consistency and uniformity to the space.

4 A shaped path adds interest and visual stimulation to a garden. Here, warm-coloured, Flemish brick paving setts attractively offset the dense, pretty planting, which includes a white peony (see case study, p78).

The interplay of screens and paths makes for a very useable space. Semi-transparent screens stand to attention while slabs of natural stone allow the user to pause. The bearded *Iris* 'Action Front' (in pots, right) link tonally to the screens.

The Daily Telegraph Garden, Andy Sturgeon, 2010

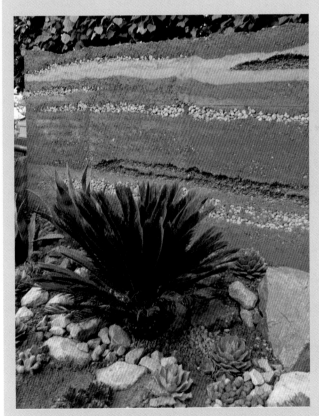

EXPERT TIP

Adam Frost
Rammed earth walls

❛ Though it has seen a revival in recent years, this method of walling construction is an ancient one – the materials having been available to humans longer than any other. Added to that is the fact that they are naturally available, which gives the walls very good green credentials, so why not try creating one in your garden. Typically, a rammed earth wall is 30–35cm (12–14in) thick. It can be constructed using form work (usually timber), which is set up to create the desired shape. Make the walls from a damp material (mixed soil, water and lime), filled on average 20cm (8in) at a time and then compacted with a power tamper. Repeat this process until the wall has reached the desired height. At this point, remove the form work and seal the wall to prevent water penetrating the materials. ❜

Rammed earth walls can make a dramatic backdrop within a garden as well as demonstrating an unusual use of materials.

TAKE ON TRADITION

Many gardeners will use slabs or bricks for a pathway or patio, but the material chosen should be similar to, or at least complementary to, the adjacent architecture.

1 The small stone setts laid in repeating fan shapes are held in place by large edging setts. Evergreen planting softens the path's line.

2 The bricks here have been laid in a basket-weave formation. Their colour variation adds interest and gives a randomness to the otherwise orderly paving approach.

3 Timber pergolas can be an attractive addition to a garden. They help define a path, provide a frame for climbers (such as here, white roses) and give a feeling of height. Construct a little higher than you might think, so plants hanging from the rails do not hit your head as you pass.

4 Main paths lead off from a circular passing space, with bricks laid in a running bond, but in different directions. The result is a considered, well-executed and interesting design.

Making that important entrance

How you physically enter – or indeed view – a garden can set the ambience and anticipation level for your enjoyment, so the composition is all important. A hidden glimpse over a wall or through a fence can engender an expectation of surprise or adventure, while a formal, defined and focused approach may set a predetermined tone to the space. Entrances don't always have to be obvious, however; sometimes, the more subtle examples can prove just as effective. For many gardens, though, the reality is that a garden is entered through a back door, side gate or patio doors, where views may be harder to frame or create. Because of this, thought must always be given to a sense of arrival and what design techniques could be used to enhance or augment such transitions; and what you should feel or experience as you go through the gate or door.

LOW-KEY WELCOME

Defining private space not only establishes limits but can also set the tone for the space beyond.

1 A rustic fence ties in well with the stepping stones, cobble infill and random planting beyond. All the elements (building, hard landscaping and planting) of this design work as a unified whole.

2 Ironwork railings have a traditional feel, and plants have been allowed to soften the overall effect. Designed for a banker, the shapes represent percentage symbols, proving that humour can be incorporated into any scheme.

COME ON IN

That all-important first view into a garden can be vital to the overall enjoyment of an outside area, so from the outset consider how people will physically enter your space.

1 This structured and well-proportioned garden uses a suite of traditional Swedish materials in a pared-down but considered way. A sense of 'what next?' is created by the path being staggered, and at the far end white-flowering foxgloves beckon the visitor still further.

2 This twisting, curling, arching entrance makes a bold statement as you look into the garden. Made from woven hazel, it gives an energetic feel to the space – and encourages you to walk through and experience the planting beyond. The rigid nature of its construction also gives it a solid feel.

3 The bold, Chinese-inspired moon gate entrance may be visible, but its path through is somewhat hidden by the arrangement of hard and soft materials in the foreground. Full of symbolism and meaning, the passage through the circular entrance leads to another defined area.

Many gardens at Chelsea are based on a theme – whether that be pictoral, interpretative or cerebral. The successful ones, however, work best when they are appreciated by people who may or may not know the theme – and here, Jinny Blom succeeded on both levels. This garden was not only pretty, but also well structured, balanced and meaningful. It used masses of 'soft' planting to unify the space, while including three circular shapes which together created a moon gate. This formal sculptural element was balanced beautifully by the plants and associated paving. The result was a calm, tranquil and genuine example of what you could do with a private garden of 10 x 23m (33 x 70ft) in size.

It is true to say that many, if not most, successful garden designers are influenced by other masters of their art. In this instance, the designer created a garden that paid homage to the 1950s Italian architect Carlo Scarpa. In plan, it had different areas of hard landscaping 'pads' countered by dense planting beds; the different number of routes through the garden at varying levels represented 'a journey through the shifting and unpredictable moments in life'. This may sound a little grand, but the reality was pretty close. If you wanted to search it

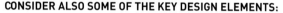

out, the symbolism of life's journey, of beginning at the front of the space in youth and ending at the back of the garden in old age, could easily be 'read'. But if not, then the planting on its own carried you along, giving visual consistency across the space.

CONSIDER ALSO SOME OF THE KEY DESIGN ELEMENTS:

- the three circular shapes (at the entrance a transparent bronze solar gate, near the middle a 'floating' lunar gate and at the back a red sandstone disc) give structure and focus throughout the garden;
- when viewed on their own, they are circular sculptures, but when observed head on (as in this photograph) they merge to create a moon gate;
- planting is very strong, with a mix of grasses and herbaceous perennials mingling to give a 'floating' atmosphere – no soil can be seen;
- edges of steps or paths appear to be invisible because of the plants around;
- the fastigiate (columnar) oaks, which play sentry to the irregular path, and dense hornbeam hedge (along the boundary) give a green backdrop to the oranges, blues, whites and pinks of the flowers;
- a rectangular, low-level, flat water feature (at the back) gives a different, more open and reflective atmosphere – perhaps symbolising maturity and age as the visitor edges ever nearer the final red sandstone disc.

1 A circular sculpture, the first of three, sets the tone for this garden. Here, the transparent bronze 'solar' gate symbolises life beginning, and it balances perfectly with the two sculptures beyond. A strong focal point can be created in any garden, and it helps the viewer orientate him- or herself throughout the space.

DESIGNER Jinny Blom

CONTRACTOR Crocus.co.uk

AWARD Gold

CATEGORY Show Garden, 2007

SPONSOR Laurent-Perrier (UK) Ltd

KEY WORDS flowery; 'floating'; informal; moon gates; focal point; relaxing

IN A SENTENCE... A clever garden that uses the concept of moon gates to give vertical structure, while the underplanting is informal and endlessly pretty.

2 Colours and textures in an endless range cover the whole space, unifying it and giving it lots of interest. In this really strong, well-planted garden, the grasses include *Stipa gigantea* and *S. tenuissima*, and the flower colour comes from orange bearded iris and *Geranium sylvaticum* 'Mayflower'.

3 Two separated circular sculptures maintain the focal point in this space: one, a 'lunar' gate suspended above a pond; the other, a solid circular sandstone disc.

4 Columnar oak trees, specifically used for tall 'accent' planting, give a subtle vertical scale; note that they also help balance the three circular sculptures. Vertical height helps trick the eye into thinking the space is bigger than it actually is, by taking the eye away from the ground plan.

5 The paved areas are set at differing 90-degree intervals, and at differing heights. Symbolically they signify the challenging transitions in life, but in reality they bring colour and practicality to the space. They make movement down the garden more surprising and they link tonally with the moon gate.

6 A tall hornbeam hedge around the boundary helps offset the planting, paving and sculptures. Its dense green allows the flower colours to be seen and helps 'frame' the whole composition.

BREWIN DOLPHIN

Managing to make a Chelsea garden have an air of permanence, a feeling that it has been around for a long time, is a special gift that only a few designers possess. By combining high quality materials with choice planting, the skill of the designer is to visually and convincingly transport you to another space, a garden that you could imagine physically owning or coming across when exploring a bigger garden. Combine that design ability with skilled craftspeople and you get a great end result.

Cleve West is just such a garden designer. He manages to create subtle, realistic detailing with choice planting and well considered hard materials, all of which are combined in a garden that gives plenty of ideas. At the crux of this space is his consideration of how you enter, pass through and look around the plot – from the tall topiary yew trees to the Cotswold stone wall. The central path allows for views left, right and straight on, and the boundary is kept in check by the beech hedging. This is simple but effective garden design in action, and can easily be translated to any domestic garden.

TAKING TIPS FROM CLEVE WEST:

- there are four main design elements to this garden: the boundary hedging, the topiary, the soft underplanting and the Cotswold stone hard-landscaping materials. The repetition of materials through the space gives a coherent feel and creates a realistic way of making a garden;
- all gardens require focal points to sustain interest, and here there are two types – the different height topiary yew columns, and at the end, an asymmetrical wall sculpture. Between them, they create spaces and open areas, allowing for planting, passing through or 'pauses' between each area;
- the clear, definite boundary (common beech has been used) creates a backdrop – like wallpapered or painted walls in a house, a boundary hedge should be used to allow the elements in front of it to be seen and enjoyed;
- mixing the planting (from mature yew trees to annual poppies) makes for seasonal interest but is also clever budgeting – by saving money on annual seed, more can be spent on permanent features such as trees or hedges;
- many garden designers talk of 'the borrowed landscape' – if you have neighbouring trees or plants that can be seen from your garden, use their visual impact to make your garden seem a lot bigger.

1 Lawns are important elements in most gardens, and the small strip of turf at the front sets off the planting so well. The low retaining wall cuts through the planting and allows people to step up, and into, the garden.

2 One of the most striking focal points is the vertical, wall-hung sculpture. Originally the top of an old well head, its asymmetrical shape links to the rest of the stonework throughout the garden and offers, with its hole in the centre, a sense of depth.

DESIGNER Cleve West

CONTRACTOR Steve Swatton

AWARD Gold, Best in Show

CATEGORY Show Garden, 2012

SPONSOR Brewin Dolphin

KEY WORDS traditional; yew trees; topiary; soft planting; stonework; sculpture; boundaries

IN A SENTENCE... A beautifully presented garden that has traditional design influences brought up-to-date.

3 By 'borrowing' the view of the London plane trees beyond, the garden seems a lot bigger and helps make the visitor's eye go beyond the actual plot shape. This is something that can easily be considered in a domestic garden.

4 The solidity of the yew topiary could seem over dominant in some gardens, but the informal, 'frothy' underplanting softens the effect and allows them to look grounded in the site. Each one is a different height from the next, and at between 25–35 years old, they are a very special addition to any space.

5 The underplanting around the space is a mix of some beautiful plants – including different types of allium bulbs (white *Allium stipitatum* 'Mount Everest' and purple *Allium atropurpureum*), annual pink-flowered corncockle (*Agrostemma githago*) and dark claret red perennial *Aquilegia vulgaris* 'Ruby Port'.

6 Tall stone pillars in the front third of the garden hold beautiful gates that give a formal entrance to the space. By the addition of sculptures at the top, your eye extends upwards and onwards to the trees beyond – a clever trick to make the garden look a lot bigger than it actually is.

PLANTING

The plants really are the stars
in any garden and at Chelsea
this is definitely the case:
they provide the colour, drama
and excitement that engages
gardeners at all levels.

For many people, Chelsea is about the plants and, as Chelsea is a flower show, it would be unimaginable for flowers not to take pride of place. Whether rare or unusual, in the Great Pavilion or show gardens, they often 'make' the gardens. From modernist designs using lines of hedges to cottage-garden combinations crowded with irises or roses, Chelsea's displays satisfy the need to be inspired.

The RHS Chelsea Flower Show sets the tone for the gardening year. It feels like the start of the season, even though most people will already have started growing seed and establishing plants. Being confronted by the colour and combinations of the plants on display makes you yearn for the summer ahead.

Yet, among this exuberance it is worth having a reality check. Not every type of plant can be shown in late spring – those that flower in autumn or winter can't be fooled into thinking May is their natural flowering time. And, in addition, not everything at Chelsea is as nature intends. Some dazzling combinations are artificially contrived,

and certain plants would never grow together in the open ground; correct planting distances are usually ignored so as to stage a stronger display; and what is on show is often protected from the vagaries of weather. These factors shouldn't undermine the displays, but they are best viewed with open eyes.

So, what can be seen? Cottage-garden abundance with endless colour; swathes of prairie-style planting; crisp lines of contemporary combinations; and trees and shrubs that give structure and maturity. This list could go on for pages, but essentially Chelsea's planting can be experienced in three broad categories: the Pavilion's floral displays; planting 'scenes' within the Pavilion; and the show gardens. The floral displays are an opportunity to see horticulture at its best and individual plants at their peak. From roses to lilies, sweet peas to *Verbascum*, the showmanship is exceptional. The same is true of the Pavilion's 'scenes', where exhibitors show combinations of plants and suggest how these plants could be grown outside. And finally, there are the show gardens which use plants to create an inspiring effect, often for visual drama or to impart a meaning (such as ideas for shady corners). These gardens can include trees or aquatic plants, shrubs or meadows, perennials or vegetables.

One of the most fascinating aspects of Chelsea is the way growers coax plants to perform, especially when displaying in The Great Pavilion. From daffodils that have been kept in cold storage to delay bud-burst to

1 Trees provide maturity and structure in show gardens, as well as a sense of scale.

2 Mixing colours and textures is crucial for visual interest. Here, evergreen *Viburnum rhytidophyllum* is the backdrop to silver-leaved *Stachys byzantina*, rounded balls of *Allium* and purple spires of *Salvia*, which combine to strong effect.

summer-flowering dahlias that have been forced to flower early, both require great skill. This isn't just about manipulating growing conditions; it requires planning and precision to ensure the growing requirements over the annual life cycle of that plant are mimicked. Some last-minute techniques are often required: for example, hair dryers are used to open up a flower bud and foam coffee cups can be placed over flowers to protect them from

the rain. There are hundreds of such tricks. So what does all this passion and skill produce? Many people talk of plant trends coming from Chelsea. In some years, a certain colour such as purple or green might dominate; in other years, there is a reliance on texture or leaf shape. Often plants such as *Allium*, bearded iris, *Aquilega* or umbellifers will steal the show. Alternatively it may be a dazzling display of dahlias (shown for the first time in 2009) that takes the breath away. Naturally inspired planting combinations have really come to the fore in recent years, blending plants to lead the visitor's view through and across the space; purple *Allium* flowers, nodding *Stipa gigantea* grass and spires of herbaceous perennials are now popular design techniques.

Planting can also reflect the mood of society or follow fashion: Tom Stuart-Smith's garden in 2008 (see case study, p78) led the way in muted tones, perhaps reflecting social uncertainty in the economy at that time. New techniques include green roofs, vertical planting on walls and ornamental meadows. Whether you are a new gardener or experienced visitor, the display of plants at Chelsea will give you an opportunity to stop and indulge in this melting pot of horticultural splendour, blended with a large dose of showmanship. Who could ask for more?

3 This clean contemporary design uses just one genus – a succulent, *Sempervivum* – and relies on the interplay between plant form and container style to provide interest.

4 The thin tree trunks rise nicely out of the planting below – the soft blue *Meconopsis* poppies and the dark purple of the *Aquilega* 'Black Barlow' are a beautiful combination.

1

A modern tale

When describing design, many commentators and designers use the word 'modern' to reflect a contemporary style that, in essence, is about an apparent simpleness in planting combinations: maybe a few species of plants have been used, or the same plant repeated within a space. However, the visual result can often belie the intricate nature of the planting and the complexity of selecting the plants. Appropriate plant choice is essential for a scheme if it is to hold together, especially if more contemporary hard materials, sculpture or furniture are to be used. Consider planting in blocks or swathes, and remember that foliage and texture are as important as flower colour and seasonal variation. With a little planning, modern planting design can be a year-round addition to any garden.

COMBINING OLD AND NEW

Although mixing different plants together is nothing new, bringing a contemporary touch to the scheme can create plantings that are timely and interesting.

1 Blocks of plants have been expertly put together, with a simple palette of green foliage and white flowers. In the foreground white *Iris* merge with the taller spires of white *Digitalis*, while white *Viburnum opulus* 'Roseum' flourishes below the birch trees.

2 Silvery, sword-like leaves of *Astelia chathamica* contrast with the burgundy dwarf bearded *Iris* in front in this modern planting scheme, where flowering and foliage plants have been intermingled.

3 Modernist-inspired planting elements work well together in this garden. They are the formal clipped box hedge, the billowing and frothy planting within, the wispy wands of grass *Stipa gigantea* nodding in the air and the raised canopy of the tree beyond.

3

ARCHITECTURAL TAKE

Putting plants with distinctive foliage or flowers together can create a bold impression.

1 The rounded heads of spring-flowering *Allium* seem to be popping out of the frothy grasses below. The two different grasses give a slightly wild, naturalistic texture to the space – as does the woven wicker fencing at the edge of the picture. The combination of brown timber, purple flowers and green grasses makes for an attractive detail of planting.

2 Rounded box (*Buxus*) balls are very popular with designers for their consistent colour and shape. Here the spheres combine with grasses and other clipped shrubs for contrasting effect.

The enduring appeal of cottage gardens

Ask most first-time, and in fact many seasoned, gardeners what their favourite style of planting is and it will probably be cottage gardens. For many decades, the appeal of plants growing together in an apparently random manner has touched the sentimental bone in most observers. There is something informal, uncontrived and undesigned about this style of planting. Yet cottage gardens require quite a lot of maintenance to ensure a

balance is achieved, as well as an understanding of how plants grow – and compete – together to have a hope of succeeding for the long term. Chelsea gardens demonstrate that this style is for the romantic in each and every one of us, allowing all to forget about colour rules or textural definition; instead, cottage garden planting encourages you to sit back and enjoy the variety and display that so often is on offer in many gardens.

CELEBRATION IN DIVERSITY

Mixing plant shapes, colours and habits is at the core of this seemingly informal but planterly style.

1 Creamy yellow summer bedding plants, which help give that hit of summer colour, mix well with the rounded leaves of *Alchemilla mollis*, the silvery grey *Artemisia* and the burgundy-red sweet williams.

2 Even though there is a faintly contemporary feel to this garden's stone walls, the planting is decidedly informal and cottagey.

3 This quiet detail of planting along a path typifies cottage gardens, with their clumps of purple-blue *Nepeta* and *Alchemilla mollis* growing under pink sun roses (*Cistus*).

4 In this modern take on rural French planting, bearded *Iris* has been primarily used at the front of the planting area. The box (*Buxus*) balances with the wall beyond, and helps anchor the *Iris* in between.

5 The dominant reds of corn poppy (*Papaver rhoeas*) bring this scene alive, while the white-flowering umbellifer (purple-leaved cow parsley, *Anthriscus sylvestris* 'Ravenswing') is a useful colour addition.

6 Although this rustic scene is somewhat stage set, the wooden water butt, old-fashioned watering can and flowering lavender below conjure up a charming image.

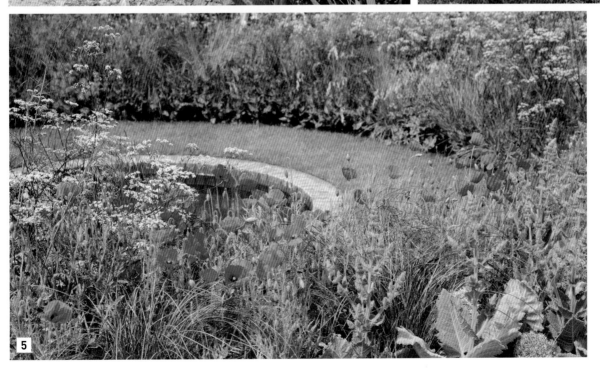

Planting for drought

How the climate changes is of substantial importance to gardeners. Whether on a seasonal level – if one summer is hotter and drier than the previous one – or on a more long-term prediction of substantial climate change, some plantings may have to be altered over the coming years. This means that if location and aspect demand it, gardeners have to respond by selecting plants that suit and thrive in the new circumstances in that area; such changes, however, don't mean that everyone will be living in Mediterranean-style gardens next year. But, if change is required, then what a choice you are faced with – thousands of plants from all over the world are now available to gardeners, with the internet assisting seed swapping as well as the constant exchange of information and learning. Thus, as the climate changes, you can learn from others, and vice versa. Chelsea designers, too, ever keen to include new or more unusual plants, offer a raft of suitable ideas to take back to your own garden.

BOLD FORM AND STRUCTURE

Plants with silvery grey leaves, or fleshy succulent foliage, are well adapted to growing in reduced rainfall areas.

1 Bold, dark green leaves of *Cycas revoluta* make a great backdrop to this light-blue selection of summer-flowering *Agapanthus*. The background palms add to a quasi-tropical and Mediterranean feel.

2 The silvery white, hairy leaves of *Verbascum* create an eye-catching visual statement. Later in the season the yellow flower spike of the *Verbascum* may extend upwards of 1m (3ft).

3 This shallow bowl has been planted with low-growing, drought-tolerant *Sempervivum* and *Echeveria* species, mulched on top with stones (to help keep available moisture in the soil). Note how the spiky, purple-leaved *Cordyline* behind continues the colour theme.

4 Sedum matting, which is often used for creating green roofs (see p169), here welcomes random plantings of silvery blue and burgundy *Sempervivum*.

5 Although tender *Agave americana* 'Mediopicta Alba' will not survive outside during winters in cool-temperate regions, it does provide a stunning display in summer, given good drainage. Watch out for the spines, however, which can be very painful.

1

1

Formality and grandeur

Something about formal planting schemes transcends fashions and time. There is a consistency to their use and application in a garden that cleverly allows formal-style planting to be interpreted from historical recreation all the way through to contemporary style. And it is this ability to morph into the required overall design that makes formal plantings so popular in Chelsea show gardens. In essence, such a style includes clipped box, rows of trees, 'seas' of green and repetition of form or colour. The beauty of the planting is its simpleness, supported by the apparent control humans have over the land; there is little room or time for impromptu planting here. Such formal gardens may leave some people with a feeling that the garden is bland and regimented; but for many others it is a stylish way to design a garden – whether at Chelsea or at home.

ALL SHAPES AND SIZES

Plant selection is crucial to ensure that a formal planting scheme can be created – and maintained – in the appropriate style.

1 This substantial garden uses a range of formal techniques to sublime effect. The large blocks of box (*Buxus*) echo the linearity of the paving, while the trees give the space a cool feel; they also add height and make the area feel much bigger than it actually is. The trees are *Schinus molle*, which are subtropical and therefore not hardy in cool-temperate areas, and more hardy *Trachycarpus fortunei* palms.

2 White trunks of birch establish a feeling of a mini copse, and visually link into the white walls and white garden building at the rear. Low-growing *Rodgersia* produces a blanket of green leaves, enhanced by creamy white flowers atop.

3 *Pinus sylvestris* 'Watereri' brings an unusual texture and colour to this garden and introduces a low hummocky feel to the area, especially when it is this tightly pruned. It is an unusual, yet totally successful planting choice.

4 Full on formality reigns here. The form of this standard pruned juniper – an unusual selection for a container – is repeated by neighbouring, tightly clipped specimens. Beware though: sometimes, too much of the same shape can be a little too repetitive, especially in a restricted space. The juniper is surrounded by *Soleirolia soleirolii*.

Colour themed

When talking to gardeners about the main role they need planting to achieve in their garden, the most common response is that it should provide some colour, whether it be clashing hues that slide and collide, or a restrained palette of just one colour consistently used. Although foliage and flower colours are a deeply personal choice, the prevailing fashion suggests that these should be harmonious rather than contradictory. Whatever the range of colours being chosen, they should work together and not end up causing a visual headache. This doesn't mean that all schemes should include soft pastels and shades – far from it. Bold and brash are often seen at Chelsea, but even then they are introduced with consideration. Colour can be added in myriad ways, whether via flower colour throughout a season or by changing foliage tones over a year. The show gardens display a snapshot of colour ideas, and it is up to individual gardeners to experiment with their own take at home.

FULL-ON COLOUR FOR FULL-ON EFFECT

Whether foliage or flower power, plants must be considered for the colour contribution they offer.

1 Blending soft colours together can give a relaxed and feminine feeling to a garden: for example, red-flowering *Geum* mixes well with lime-green and yellow *Alchemilla mollis*.

2 Yellow dominates in this informal planting combination of moisture-loving plants. These include yellow-flowering *Zantedeschia*, the curly leaves of a sedge behind and the orange-yellow flowers of *Geum*. The result is a neat little planted area.

3 Colour shapes can be created in any garden by using plants in an eye-catching and massed way. Here the designers have balanced rectangles of lawn turf with slabs of red-leaved *Heuchera* 'Peach Flambé'. In winter, the heuchera will die down so the effect would be significantly reduced.

4 A beautiful blend of planting makes for a tapestry of colour and texture. White flower heads of *Allium nigrum* intermingle with the flat yellow discs of *Achillea* 'Taygetea'; the frothy leaves of fennel (*Foeniculum vulgare* 'Purpureum') contrast with the silvery leaves of *Artemisia ludoviciana*. The round, purple heads of *Allium cristophii* also bring shape and form to the composition.

EXPERT TIP

Tom Stuart-Smith
Layered planting

❛The idea behind layered planting in the garden is to repeat the ecological patterns inherent in complex plant communities. In an oak woodland, for example, there are various different levels: an upper canopy; often a middle canopy of medium-sized trees and saplings; a shrub layer; a herb layer; and then bulbs and corms at the bottom. By adapting this natural pattern to a garden, it is possible to have different layers flowering at different times, usually with the lower layers flowering first.❜

Using a range of plant types, such as bulbs, perennials, grasses and shrubs, builds up layers of interest and gives structure to your planting.

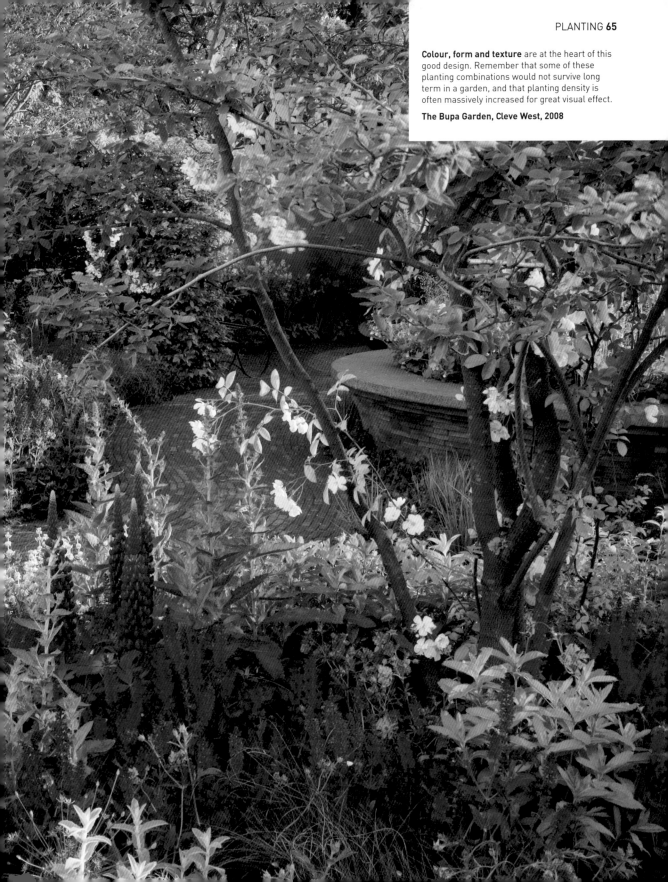

Colour, form and texture are at the heart of this good design. Remember that some of these planting combinations would not survive long term in a garden, and that planting density is often massively increased for great visual effect.

The Bupa Garden, Cleve West, 2008

Simplicity in minimalism

In a way, minimal planting is similar to formal planting schemes. A considered and ordered view of how to use growing material is required where each subject must warrant its inclusion based on leaf shape, overall habit, flower colour or year-round appearance. In addition, the planting must be in tune with the overall design theme, maybe referencing or supporting a colour, texture or implied meaning. What may look stunning and at the peak of growth at Chelsea, however, can be quite different in the home garden. Minimalism demands an order and exactitude of plant choice that many gardeners may find limiting, because of their desire to have a diversity in plant selection as well as year-round interest. Fortunately, in the appropriate place, and with the right planting, the style can be a sublime addition to any garden space.

1

ONE OF A KIND

Using just a single species of plant is frequently a great way to undertake a minimal design.

1 Low-growing mounds of *Festuca gautieri* seem to cut through the granite wedges either side of this bed and give the impression of a naturally occurring rock and plant community.

CLEAN AND SIMPLE

Careful plant selection is crucial to the success of minimalistic planting schemes.

1 The billowing and ever-changing shapes of grass *Stipa tenuissima* contrast well against the tightly clipped form of the box (*Buxus*) balls behind.

2 Young, silvery grey leaves of *Verbascum* are beautifully offset by the white-flowering, scented biennial stock (*Matthiola incana*) behind. Note how this duo also complements the silvery grey of the granite boulder in the foreground. The *Verbascum* has been planted densely here for show-stopping effect but not for long-term, sustainable plant growth.

3 Massed plantings of one plant type are often seen at Chelsea. This close-up view of bearded iris shows off the flower and leaf shape in great detail.

Planting with wildlife in mind

Although it is clear that the plants selected for any garden should be chosen as a response to the owner's wishes, the role that plant selection can have on wildlife should also be considered. A good range of plants – whether grown for foliage (such as conifers) or for flowers (such as summer bedding) – is best for a balanced sustainable garden that welcomes, and is home to, a broad range of wildlife. Current research is now finding that wildlife needs a diverse range of plant type (bulbs, annuals, herbaceous perennials, shrubs, evergreens, long grass, trees and so on); in addition, many animals and insects don't seem to worry whether plants are native or non-native. Gardeners, therefore, are in a unique position to help attract wildlife to their space, no matter where it is situated. Whether your garden is extensive or minute, wildlife and planting must go hand in hand.

SOMETHING FOR ALL

Planting with wildlife in mind should lead to a greater understanding of the potential gardeners can bring to increasing biodiversity.

1 A range of living and inanimate objects occupies this 'living tower'. The succulent plants are able to withstand limited root depth and reduced amounts of irrigation, while the old sticks and twigs offer a place for creatures. The combination is a decorative, unusual but highly effective home for wildlife.

2 A field of green wheat gives the impression of an agrarian landscape and imparts a strong message of rural stewardship and organic crop production. A show garden such as this demonstrates that planting at Chelsea concerns more than just the role of ornamental plants.

3 By combining both edible and ornamental plants (kale, parsley and lettuces with tulips), different colours and textures have been brought together in a small space.

4 This standard vine has been underplanted with an array of annual wild flowers, including annual *Chrysanthemum*, typical of California meadow planting. The colour is spectacular and a significant addition to any garden.

3

4

EXPERT TIP
Nigel Dunnett
Drought-tolerant planting

❝ This type of planting is about making the right choice of plants as well as creating the appropriate growing conditions for them. Growing plants 'hard' – in free-draining soils that have had very little organic matter incorporated, and at closer spacings than might normally be considered – will make them tough, stress tolerant and naturally better able to withstand harsh conditions. Good, reliable, drought-tolerant plants that all work well in a naturalistic mix together include *Dianthus carthusianorum*, *Stachys byzantina*, *Erodium manescavii*, *Oenothera macrocarpa*, *Sedum telephium* 'Purple Emperor', *Limonium platyphyllum*, *Gaura lindheimeri*, *Phlomis russeliana*, *Stipa tenuissima* and *Verbascum phoeniceum*. ❞

[left] The bold leaves of succulent (and therefore drought-tolerant) *Agave americana* give a strong focal point to this planting.

[below left] Bright pink flowers of *Erodium manescavii* bring a vivid and warm feeling to the front of the border.

[below] This silver-leaved *Stachys*, which survives substantial drought and heat, is neatly contained by this attractive edging. Its sprawling habit would otherwise eventually envelop the path.

A nod to a natural style

The naturalistic planting style has been gaining pace over the last 15 years or so. In its loosest form, it involves designing with plants that mimic associations and styles found in nature – but by using ornamental cultivated plants rather than only natives. Thus, many schemes will include swathes of plants growing together, seeming to entwine as they might in nature. This style is relatively easy to recreate – if you have the space – but beware that even though it may look impromptu it does take substantial foresight and skill to achieve. One of the primary concerns is that of how the plants will grow together over time; the gardener needs to monitor and intervene (if necessary) to ensure a balance is maintained. Chelsea gardens provide great ideas for naturalistic planting, but if recreating them in your garden be sure to know what plants you are selecting and how they will develop.

ALL IN THE MIX

A range of flowering and foliage plants can combine to produce a naturalistic feel in a planting scheme.

1 The success of this combination underlines the link between ground-level planting, mature trees, the confines of a well-trimmed hedge, and the garden building peaking into view on the far left. In the foreground, bearded *Iris* 'Dutch Chocolate' mirrors the vertical accents of the foxgloves; the beautiful, informal frothy purple foliage and white flowers of *Anthriscus sylvestris* 'Ravenswing' weave throughout the space underneath the multi-stemmed *Parrotia persica* trees.

2 A mass of white *Geranium phaeum* **'Album'**, flanked on the right by spires of white *Digitalis*, lead the garden visitor's eye through the space, to the silver birch tree trunks beyond.

3 Yellow-and-white wetland *Iris* exude light and colour in this planting area, which borders and provides definition to the paving to the left. The different flower and leaf shapes make an overall impression similar to combinations found in nature.

4 Rivers of colour and texture abound in this show garden, but a large space would be needed in a home garden to achieve such a result. Its blend of silver-leaved *Stachys byzantina*, the purple rounded heads of *Allium*, the purple spires of *Salvia* and the creamy yellow *Achillea* beyond conjure an almost prairie feel. The bold dash of red in the centre brings a natural disharmony to the scene.

Containers for all gardens

As garden design has developed over the years, so too have the products and artefacts to support it. Containers and planters are no exception to this evolution. By using improved manufacturing techniques and new materials, a wealth of ideas has been developed for containers. In addition to this, increasing plant availability and choice have meant a wider range of species can be grown in planters. Containers, however, are man-made environments, so you must consider your plant choice carefully as well as each plant's ability to grow in a restricted space and whether you can maintain the effect you desire. There are practical considerations, too, when planting in containers. Good-quality potting compost must be used; feeding, especially during periods of strong growth, must be done; water-retaining gel can be used; and watering, even in times of rain, should be monitored and checked.

EYE-CATCHING STATEMENTS

Dramatic planters can be used as really strong design statements in a garden, but ensure plants can live happily with their bedfellows.

1 This unusual scheme by a Japanese designer used a series of large 'containers' at different levels to accentuate the form and texture of each plant. The same plants have been grouped in each planter, helping reinforce a bold but restrained vision of a contained garden.

2 The bright summer colour of *Calendula* lifts this corner of the garden, while the massive container plays a supporting but defining role.

3 A contemporary feel is created by linking plants to hard materials. White peonies are planted in tall, white planters while uplighters bring the space to life at night all within the straight lines of the paving.

1

2

NO NEED FOR PLANTS

Not all planters or containers have to be filled with plants. Sometimes their beauty can be appreciated better when they are left empty.

1 A glazed urn has been placed on its side to reduce its overall impact, while the flowering *Rhododendron* around it helps to give context – and a focal point – to the scene.

2 The asymmetrical curved shape of this container allows for it to become a statement piece in a small corner of the garden. Its white colour is mirrored in the surrounding planting, and sits comfortably with the green foliage either side.

EXPERT TIP
Tom Stuart-Smith
Cloud pruning

❛ 'Cloud pruning' is a brilliantly expressive term as it describes the process exactly, that is, pruning any plant to resemble a cumulus in its full buxom splendour. This technique is normally done on box and yew. The idea of cloud pruning a tree is based on the Japanese tradition of Niwaki, in which the tree is pruned to reveal and accentuate its essential form and branch structure. When used *en masse*, cloud pruning can give a slightly surreal and dreamy impression. ❜

When trimming plants, swivel-blade hand shears are useful for giving a precise finish – in this case, to a box (*Buxus*) ball.

Cloud pruning is not an easy task, and takes years of dedicated pruning and foresight to achieve such an end result. Mature examples such as this, however, can be found for sale in garden centres.

SUCCESS IN SIMPLICITY

Often just one or two types of plants can be used to great effect in some schemes; thus, less can be better than more in a container.

1 Basket-weave terracotta pots have been planted with pink-purple *Osteospermum* (on the left) and silver-leaved *Convolvulus cneorum* (on the right). When viewed in combination with the planting surrounding them, they make a great overall garden scene.

2 Bay is a popular choice for many gardeners, as its evergreen leaves provide year-round foliage, plus it can also be easily shaped or trained. Here the trunks have been twisted slightly for a spiral effect.

3 This old washing tub makes a good base for an alpine-type display, filled with *Sempervivum* and stones. These succulents are great for containers as they need little additional watering.

4 Clean and stark planters, filled with a white mulch, are welcome homes to *Libertia grandiflora*, the tall white flower spires of which give an elegance and stature to the display.

5 In this great fun and sustainable way to recycle an old item, succulents (*Sempervivum* and *Echeveria* selections) almost take over the old tool box. The pretty flowering stems of the *Echeveria* seem to dance in the air.

5

Some show gardens are so visionary in their design, and so well executed, that they live up to their hype. At the heart of this huge garden was the notion that urban spaces can be both beautiful and productive – if only people considered the value of producing food locally. Its creators claimed that 'food in London would run out in four days if supplies ceased', so everything here was edible – from low growing herbs to salad window boxes on the tower.

One of the garden's most interesting aspects is the stark use of strong horizontal and vertical lines. At the back, the tower looms up over ten metres; a screen housing endless 'insect hotels' sits in the lee of the tower; and to the left, pleached limes (*Tillia europaea* 'Pallida') continue the vertical accent. In contrast, 'table-pruned' mulberry trees (*Morus alba* 'Platanifolia') and dense planting below accentuate the horizontal. The space feels much bigger; the texture of the vegetation is contrasted; and the 'hard' structures are softened.

OTHER REASONS WHY THIS IS SUCH A GOOD DESIGN:
- materials are selected carefully, from the textured planting on ground level to the smooth, metallic tower, and the varied insect-house materials;
- environmental awareness is at its heart, with rainwater harvesting and storage, solar panels and a wind turbine on the top of the tower;
- this space shows just how calming different shades of grey and green can be – from the leaves on the trees to the painted steel on the side of the tower; it makes for a softer and more tactile space, qualities much needed in a city;
- often in gardens, the view outside of your perimeter can be unpleasant or unwanted, so by careful placement of trees, structures or ornaments, unsightly views can be blocked out – this garden does just that, by concentrating the pleached lime, insect hotel and tower in the corner, blocking out a neighbouring view;
- in a limited space, make every plant count: as the designers have here, use edible plants ornamentally, whether in the ground or on a wall – don't hold back in maximising the return from your outside space, especially in urban areas.

DESIGNER Laurie Chetwood and Patrick Collins

CONTRACTOR Willerby Landscapes

AWARD Gold

CATEGORY Show Garden, 2011

SPONSOR B&Q

KEY WORDS urban ideas; tower; green walls; shade planting; edibles; biodiversity; community gardens

IN A SENTENCE... An enticing vision for how we could all live in shared urban spaces, whether for growing ornamentals or edibles.

1 Rising at the back of the space is the 'tower' (imagine it symbolising any building that can be found in any town or city) which was four storeys high. By adding large window boxes to the end (growing herbs, vegetables and fruit in them) and clothing the rest of the façade in a mix of chamomile, golden oregano and three different types of thyme, the designers have reduced the visual bulk of the tower while making it a productive and useful planting space.

2 The rooms of the 'insect hotel' were made by school children and members of a youth club – they used a range of recycled materials from cardboard to straw, plastic pipes to old pieces of wood. These spaces allow a host of wildlife to set up home and be a place of sanctuary and life for urban biodiversity – supported also by a range of planting, much of which was pollinator-friendly.

3 'Table pruned' trees (here a mulberry, *Morus alba* 'Platanifolia') are often expensive to buy at this mature size, but they can provide a wonderful visual treat while giving shade from the sun. Another benefit is that they also stop views into a space from prying eyes next door – especially if overlooking windows are higher than your ground floor.

4 Shade is often forgotten about in gardens, but it can be essential during summer especially in urban areas. Consider how and where you want your shade to fall, and choose your planting and hard materials accordingly.

5 By mixing ornamental plants (here a crimson rose, *Rosa* 'Burgundy Ice') with herbs (such as blue-flowered borage and flowering lavender, *Lavandula angustifolia*), the planting palette is not only beautiful but useful too – all of the plants in the garden have some association with food or drink.

THE LAURENT-PERRIER GARDEN

There is often a temptation to include too many colours or 'elements' in a garden, in a vain attempt to make it look more exciting. This one is a successful essay in how to do the complete opposite. Simple textures, a range of form and plant shape, and a repetitious use of the colour green, are bisected by rectangular paving setts and raised zinc tanks of water. The design balances masses (planting, water troughs) and voids (spaces between trees, paths), and allows the entity to work as one while still giving discrete areas for walking or sitting. The result is a cool, subtle and pared-down statement of what a garden can be.

Tom Stuart-Smith is a well-known Chelsea designer who always manages to succeed in creating awe-inspiring show gardens, as he also does for his many private clients. He described this grove as 'a contemplative space with a dreamy, slightly surreal character'... and with good reason.

CONSIDER THE QUALITY OF THIS SPACE:

- the cool and constant 'base notes' of the groundcovering greens, in leaf shape and flower form;
- the sporadic punctuation of white flowers;
- trimmed, 30-year-old, 'cloud-pruned' hornbeams that give height, maturity and structure;
- a seemingly random planting pattern held within organic border shapes;
- water features, an end wall and paving that bring man-made materials to an otherwise planterly space.

At home, such refined choices might be difficult to make – you need a focused planting palette and a high level of maintenance to keep the consistency that is shown in this photograph. Also, much of this planting would die down during winter months. Remember this garden was on display for only six days, not six months or even six years! However, it shows how less can often mean more: with some choice (and often expensive) focal points (here, hornbeam trees and water features), and with a matrix of planting underneath softening the effect, a garden of calm and the designer's slight 'surrealism' can be achieved.

Seemingly random planting in this cool and contemplative garden gives a lush informal feel (left). It is protectively watched over by cloud-pruned hornbeams – dominating but also framing the space. The zinc troughs of water – from a distance looking black and bottomless – bring an extra dimension.

1 These zinc tanks are a perfect example of high-quality detailing adding to the overall effect of a garden. A small gap between the surface level of the water and the edge of the tanks allows water to spill over and recirculate. The gap is consistent; the water is level (and black lined which helps give a feeling of 'the unknown'); and the combination of colours (black and silver) is contemporary and complementary. Such sublime detailing helps any garden exude a feeling of quality and longevity.

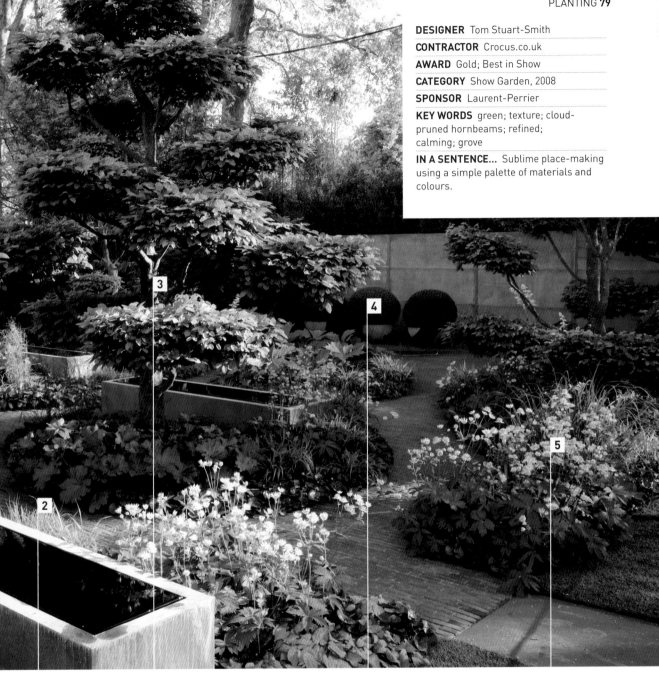

DESIGNER Tom Stuart-Smith

CONTRACTOR Crocus.co.uk

AWARD Gold; Best in Show

CATEGORY Show Garden, 2008

SPONSOR Laurent-Perrier

KEY WORDS green; texture; cloud-pruned hornbeams; refined; calming; grove

IN A SENTENCE... Sublime place-making using a simple palette of materials and colours.

2 Looking along the linear Flemish paving setts of the path you can see how the proportion of the planting either side neither dominates nor underwhelms – the balance is spot on. This garden is a lesson in what should go into, and stay out of, a designed space.

3 Trees cloud-pruned within a centimetre of their lives give a rounded and structural feel to the garden. This sculptural, large-scale bonsai treatment adds to the densely planted, green grove. If you were to try this at home, it would take you decades to achieve; if you want the look, it may be best to blow the budget and buy mature examples like these, but they aren't your normal garden-centre finds.

4 Three oversized domes of box (*Buxus*) in containers give a regimented but defined feel to the back wall – and a sense of form and structure for the visitor to look towards – among all the greenery and seamless planting in this garden.

5 The combination of small rounded leaves of *Asarum europaeum* near to wide-leaved, toothed rodgersias, white-flowering astrantias, small-leaved hostas and other groundcovering plants creates a mainly green, textural and dense vegetative design.

OUTDOOR LIVING

The possibilities for living how you want, in your garden, are truly endless.

Most people who are interested in gardening, in whatever form, enjoy being outdoors whether it is for nurturing unusual types of plants or sharing a glass of wine with friends, for giving children the opportunity to run amok or for walking around an arboretum full of enormous trees. It is unsurprising therefore that the concept of 'outdoor living' is so firmly rooted in people's minds.

In the garden design world, the term 'outdoor living' loosely covers dining areas, patios, decks, outdoor kitchens, spaces for the kids to play and so on. However, if Chelsea and the other gardening shows across the world teach us one thing, it is that gardening is one of the most diverse pastimes you can find. Just as everyone is different, so too are their gardens – and their 'outdoor living' space.

But what Chelsea does better than most shows, perhaps, is demonstrate just what you may want from your space. In essence, it concerns anything that you might see built or sitting in your garden – from outdoor kitchens to concealed lighting, from exterior paint to shade structures. This chapter specifically focuses on elements such as buildings, unusual features, seating and changing uses of your garden. (In reality, of course, elements such as paving, entrances, paths and walls would also be included, but these are dealt with in a previous chapter.)

At its largest, outdoor living considers the role of garden buildings, as well as more subtle garden structures. Garden rooms, whether wooden summerhouses or brick-built architectural statements, have always been part of a garden's recipe, but only in the past 20 or 30 years has there been an explosion of design style and material choice. Designers now create their own garden room or structure to sit in harmony with the overall design. For gardeners, many similar buildings are available to purchase from specialist firms. Equally, if your taste and budget are less flamboyant, then sheds, summerhouses, greenhouses and other garden rooms can be made by a competent builder, or put together by a DIY enthusiast.

Garden features, on the other hand, seem to be a whole new design development. They work in so many ways that not even designers can really define them, but their benefit is often undoubted. Some may be small pods for sitting or resting in; others may provide a subtle amount of shading; a few may be physical entities that help frame a view or the overall design. More often than not such features are used in a contemporary, modern, quite pared-down way, but that should not restrict your imagination. In a domestic setting, for example, you may think that an awning hanging above your patio doors is a little dated, and that a large patio umbrella is not big enough. The garden structure you may end up with could be a hybrid between a pergola joined to a horizontal trellis but made out of painted metal. It is features such as these

1 The shape of the cubed seats relates well to the box hedging surrounding them. Such a relationship between plants and built structures is vital.

2 For many people, gardens are for relaxing in. Seating therefore is essential and must not only be comfortable but also visually link in with the overall design.

3 If a particular style or culture inspires you, then consider all elements from planting to seating, containers to wall colour. The more authentic these elements are, the more convincing the end result.

4 'Outdoor rooms' are increasingly being created by designers, either as guest rooms, work spaces or play areas for children. Their architecture, as is so well achieved here, must be thought through carefully.

that are really exciting – you can't always put your finger on what they are or exactly what they do, but you know that the design would be a lot weaker without them.

From individual chairs that blend into the background through to bold and dramatic 'design statements', where and how you sit is an essential part of anyone's use of their outside space. Something that has really developed in recent years, however, has been the outdoor sofa (see p90) – or even 'sun bed'.

Increasingly, gardeners are considering climate change. Nowhere is this more true than in the creations from Fleming's Nurseries of Australia, whose outdoor kitchens (with integral barbecue and cooker; see case study, p100) give a taster as to what would be possible if climate change became particularly advanced for cool-temperate gardeners.

So what does this range of outdoor living examples provide? It demonstrates inspiration and ideas. It shows that if you need a building in your back yard, why not do something different. It shows that if you want new materials, then get thinking. But above all it gives people confidence to try techniques, combinations and styles that they may not be aware of. Much of this wouldn't have been possible without Chelsea leading the way, showing what can be done in the garden. The possibilities for living how you want, in your garden, are truly endless.

Sitting pretty, sitting well

Out of all the hard landscaping elements considered for a garden, seating is perhaps of most significant value. A comfortable seat, whether for an individual or for many, can help a garden visitor truly relax in an outside space, reinforcing the relationship between gardener and garden. The location, style, material and size of the seats must be appropriate to the garden in general, and can be temporary or long-term, home-made or shop-bought. Bear in mind also the demands of seat maintenance and upkeep, and practical issues of mowing regimes or surrounding planting. Seating comes in all shapes and sizes, so there should always be something for every garden. In addition to more conventional seating, bespoke and off-the-shelf benches are possible, especially for the more social gardeners, allowing more people to enjoy the garden space.

BLENDING INTO THE BACKGROUND

Not all seats need be bold or obvious; sometimes the really successful ones have a supporting role.

1 A simple wooden bench sits quietly in some dense planting, and offers an area of respite for the garden visitor from which to contemplate the plants and water feature beyond.

2 These chairs complement the overall design of the garden, blending pretty planting with rustic hard landscaping materials, as well as giving the impression of a romantic, cottage-garden outside space.

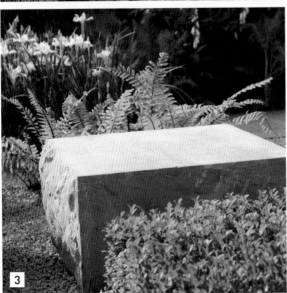

STATEMENT CHAIRS

Whether introduced singly or in pairs, chairs are a crucial element in the outside space.

1 These semi-transparent chairs by furniture designer Charlie Davidson bring a great touch to this garden. The 'river' of cut birch trunks in the foreground lends a contrasting textural element while adding height and movement to the space.

2 White mesh 'daisy'-like seats bring some humour and visual interest to this garden. Their transparent nature makes the space feel bigger.

3 This large stone plinth, cut smooth on the top and left textured on its side, acts both as a seat and as a physical mass between planting.

4 Complementing the Chinese style of this show garden, the designer has allocated this quiet corner for resting and drinking tea.

This outdoor pavilion oozes a calm and private ambience. The contemporary chairs on the patio are dominated by a circular 'window' looking onto tropical planting. An orange bromeliad adds a splash of colour to the monochrome design.

Trailfinders Australian Garden presented by Fleming's, Scott Wynd, 2010

1

2

Benches for different uses

The facility for more than one person to sit down and enjoy a garden is increasingly being explored (see also p90). For this, benches are becoming important and now comprise a significant proportion of garden furniture, welcoming as they are for conversation, lying on or making a design statement. However, as can be seen in the examples illustrated here, benches are also becoming integral to the built form of the garden, whether as visual 'relief' to planting, part retaining wall or as artworks in their own right. The upshot is that the bench so often associated with public parks or bus shelters is long gone – now is the age of new ideas, whatever your requirements.

3

SHARP AND STRAIGHT

Linear benches add more than just a place to sit in a garden; they provide a strong design statement, too.

1 These black timber benches not only create a physical barrier between path and planting, but also add texture and colour to this attractive scene.

2 A solid limestone, L-shaped bench defines the corner of this urban garden while providing a well-sized seating facility.

3 This timber cantilevered bench is a great idea for a small garden: it is comfortable and attractive, and the space underneath allows for shade-loving plants to establish.

PART OF THE PLAN

For a scheme's ultimate success it is often important to consider how and where your bench will reside in a garden.

1 These repeating benches are a bold move, but add a sense of symmetry, as well as contrasting the black colour with white walls.

2 This circular wood and stone bench cleverly reinforces the circular design of the decking; the multi-stemmed silver birch 'copse' gives a backdrop to the seating and a sense of enclosure.

3 Benches can be pieces of art in their own right. Here, the designer has blended the practical requirement of somewhere to sit with the artistic desire to link the bench visually into the overall design idea.

Taking your sofa outside

As Chelsea designers have looked further afield for inspiration, so too have they developed new ideas. One such is the advent of the garden 'sofa' – not always technically a sofa, but certainly a seating device that has the traits of settee, day bed or lounging area. The sofa concept is to encourage gardeners to relax, use and surround themselves with their plants or a view; the upshot, however, is a great conduit for conversation and entertainment. The reality for many gardeners is that they may not have enough space to incorporate such a feature, plus there is the realistic practicality of taking the cushions in and out when dodging poor weather. Yet, when executed well and established in the appropriate place, sofas can make a really unusual and welcome addition to outdoor living.

EXPERT TIP
Andy Sturgeon Decking

❛Essentially there are three types of decking for gardens:

- Tropical hardwood is the most expensive material and undoubtedly looks the most sophisticated. It is also the longest lasting timber and as decking should endure for as much as 40–60 years. Apart from their initial colours, there is little to choose between the various types, which have exotic names like Ipe and Balau, although in time sunlight will turn all of them the same silvery grey.
- Pressure-treated softwood will last less than half as long as tropical hardwood but is considerably cheaper to buy. It is easier to cut and drill, so quicker to install.
- Western red cedar falls somewhere between the other two in terms of looks, quality, price and workability.

Lay boards 'smooth side up' for a superior look, especially as the grooves in decking trap dirt and can become slippery. Pressure wash decking at least once a year. Secure decking with 'lost head' screws, which 'disappear' into the wood and don't become unwanted visual features.

Hardwoods and cedar do not need preservatives; any silvering can be removed (if required) with chemicals or pressure washing and oils, and then be restored or retained by applying appropriately tinted products. Preservatives and stains can prolong the life of softwood and improve its appearance, but avoid using varnishes because they flake and peel.❜

Decking continues to be a popular choice with gardeners, making the outside space, weather permitting, useable throughout the year.

THE FURNISHING TOUCH

Outdoor sofas must suit your overall garden design and are available in all shapes and sizes.

1 Taking its inspiration directly from interior furniture designers, this scheme mimics the common domestic arrangement in a sitting room – a sofa being placed against a wall, in front of a fire, and augmented with scatter cushions.

2 This relaxing area, surrounded by soft pink busy Lizzie bedding plants, is more of a chill-out, cushioned hollow than a sofa.

3 A dedicated eating area in a garden is often required by people: here, seating for six surrounds a bespoke glass-topped, water feature table that feeds into a pool below.

4 Furniture can easily be included in a garden. Here, retaining walls enclose the outdoor sofas, allowing occupants to feel safe and secure.

This outside living space has myriad ideas: from the long sofa seat backed by the striated stone retaining walls, to the 'plug hole' water feature and the smooth interplay between water level and decking. The end result is a truly relaxing place.

Fleming's and Trailfinders Australian Garden, presented by Melbourne, Victoria, Jamie Durie, 2008

Shade and structure

Introducing a structural element to a design is common for many Chelsea designers – the built form adding an air of permanence and solidity. In a domestic garden, the addition of some type of shade or physical structure has an equally important benefit, as well as meeting that deep-seated human desire to be protected and shielded. The design of such structures can take cues from modernist buildings or Chinese tea houses, rustic ironworks or glass rooms. Sometimes the role can be practical protection; at other times it can allude to a physical presence but is in fact more about style and stage-set. The use of garden structures can be permanent or seasonal, fully functional or light hearted. Whatever end result is chosen doesn't really matter, although as a garden owner you must consider what you need this building to achieve and how its inclusion can be adapted to your site.

INTEGRITY IN STRUCTURE

Physical forms are often important parts of Chelsea gardens and, if budget and space allow, could also be in home gardens.

1 This modern design was inspired by Japanese architecture, and it features an acrylic roof and end wall that houses ceramic sculptures by Japanese artist Mari-Ruth Oda.

2 Simple white screens, used both vertically and horizontally, help to create a series of defined spaces within this garden.

3 A substantial structure, such as this, is a bold statement for any designer, but when used with conviction could be introduced into a home garden.

PERSONAL SPACE

Including areas in a garden that feel personal and 'human scale' is important for people's enjoyment.

1 This arching white garden canopy gives a somewhat futuristic feel to the patio below – the stepping-stone path, across the water, adds to the sense that this seating area is a private, reclusive space for the garden owners.

2 With its hints of Oriental gardens mixed with savannah grassland, this deck (with roof) makes for an easily replicable garden element.

3 These sunken white pods work in harmony with the mounds of planting while giving garden visitors somewhere to relax.

4 A 'rib-cage' timber hut has been cleverly used to enliven an otherwise dull corner of a garden.

Garden buildings for all styles

Installing or commissioning a garden building can be a costly exercise for a gardener, and may well include requiring planning permission and substantial earthworks. However such constraints should not undermine in any way the enormous beauty and long-term benefit a building can bring. In essence, it symbolises that the garden owner is in control of the space, that he or she means to stay there for some time. This act of permanence is a reminder of someone's love for their outside space; it is a visible commitment to their land. There are many different types of structures available, some shop-bought while others require architectural endeavour. Consider how often the structure is to be used; what it needs to deliver; and ongoing maintenance costs. Whatever your choice, its inclusion can bring a whole new energy and visual enjoyment to your outside garden.

TRADITIONAL TAKE

A range of styles and designs can link a property with its surrounding architecture or with a considered reference to days gone by.

1 Buildings such as this one form the backdrop to many a famous historical garden, and bring elegance and architectural interest that complements the surrounding planting.

2 A simple summerhouse, well painted and gentrified inside, is a realistic addition to a Chelsea garden that many gardeners would aspire to having; note the wisteria climbing up one side.

3 Although stylised and even quite kitsch, this evocation of a beach hut is well executed and could easily be accommodated in the right garden.

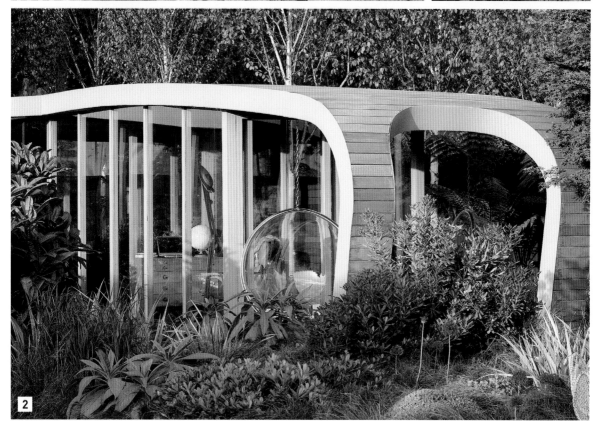

THE ROOM OUTSIDE

Actual buildings in which to house offices or guest suites are increasingly being constructed in the garden by people who want more living space.

1 Garden rooms should be practical, useful and beautiful. This contemporary summerhouse provides a great enclosed room, and has a washing line that can be folded away and hidden behind out of sight.

2 The low-slung shape and soft-toned materials used in this building allow it to bed in well with the planting in the garden – light shines into it from the glass windows, connecting inside to outside.

3 Green roofs – designed and constructed to support living plants – are increasingly being used in private and public schemes, and they help give visual garden interest as well as biodiversity a boost.

Outside space with something different

So much of gardening relates to how the individual personalises his or her outdoor space. Whether it is a certain combination of plants that reflect personal preference, or an array of materials that indicate different travels, a garden can be developed to make specific or oblique reference to the creator's desire. With this in mind, how a gardener 'decorates' the space should be considered in conjunction with any hard or soft landscaping that is needed to ensure

the desired look will still be created as the scheme nears completion. For Chelsea designers, such examples of decorative touches include bespoke sculpture, ingenious practical ideas and whimsical suggestions, and these can inspire gardeners into thinking harder about what could go into their garden. With a dash of creativity and confidence, supported by practical skills, a range of different ideas can be achieved.

5

EXPERT TIP
Bunny Guinness
Dressing the garden for a party

❛ One of the most satisfactory ways of creating a celebratory feeling is to introduce large terracotta (or other) pots with water buckets hidden inside filled with massive bouquets of flowers or with generous sprigs of greenery spiced up with any readily available flowers. Position these in prominent places to frame the front gate or door, or raise them up either side of a flight of steps for big impact. For a makeshift awning, create a loosely woven rectangle of coloured-ribbon hessian or similar and hang it between four convenient trees or partially hook it to a wall or fence; you could even rig it up on poles. This simple adornment will make any outside eating area special, however large or small. Fairy lights, cushions and candles are essential, while table runners add colour. You could also dot sprigs of cut lavender on the table. ❜

[above] Simple small details, such as this candle hanging in a jar decorated with a checked ribbon, can really help personalise a plot.

[left] Fairy lights can extend a garden's use into night-time, while adding a fun party atmosphere.

PERSONAL PREFERENCE

A range of elements can be included in a garden to respond to a gardener's aesthetic or practical needs.

1 A clever outdoor cupboard gives space for composting and recycling, and has a herb trough planted on top of it.

2 Taking the concept of the edible garden to the extreme, the designers here used every available space for growing fruit or vegetables.

3 This garden, designed for a biker, was envisaged to be situated at the back of a garage, offering a place for escape. Bike parts, oil drums and old tyres are all included in the scene.

4 Two bikes outside the front door of a house use the space efficiently and are readily accessible.

5 Even though not every garden has space for such a building, this beautiful dovecote acts as a strong focal point to the back of this space. Its colour provides relief to the shadow of the trees.

For many people across the world, living in an urban or suburban location is the norm – just in Britain alone, 85 percent of people live in a town or city. As a result, making the most of your environment, both in terms of its visual appeal and its practical use, is absolutely essential. Whether you live in Manchester or Monte Carlo, the human need to enjoy your outside space remains vital.

In this garden, designer Sarah Eberle has given a clean, modern and beautifully refined vision for how to get the most out of a small space. Her design was based on the high density living of the principality of Monaco, with its steep topography, far reaching views and the limited available space. She has achieved that subtle balance between making a space beautiful and making it useful – for example the deck path leading to the pool not only acts as a practical surface to walk on, it also houses the flowing water spout. Its overall contemporary design may not be to everyone's taste, but her vision for a beautifully designed garden stocked with plants, sculptural elements and a place to swim, has great appeal.

KEY IDEAS TO TRY FOR SMALL URBAN GARDENS:
- as space is limited, really consider what you want and where you need to have it. For example, herbs are best within arm's reach of your kitchen door, and less attractive water butts are better out of sight;
- don't limit your imagination – think about how you could plant up walls, balconies or use different containers to 'green up' your space;
- changing levels in a small space is often a good idea – with the correct positioning and material choice, it can make the space feel bigger;
- consider your climate – urban areas are often hotter and drier than the same sized space in the countryside so your plant choice can be more adventurous, such as using Mediterannean-type, drought-resistant planting;
- materially linking your garden space with the building's architecture gives a consistent and cohesive feel to your home. This can be achieved easily when starting from scratch, but if you are adding a garden onto an existing building, choose materials that complement the built form and give a visual consistency to the space.

1 For many people, having a swimming pool or plunge pool in their garden is the ultimate in luxury, but the addition of water in this garden is absolutely vital to its success – the movement, transparency and calming nature of the pool brings a totally different dimension to the space. It physically softens all the hard lines. In addition, its practical use as a place to cool down and unwind is particularly valuable in built-up and often hot urban spaces.

Designer Sarah Eberle

Contractor Peter Dowle Plants and Gardens

Award Gold

Category Show Garden, 2011

Sponsor Principality of Monaco

Key words clean lines; modern; plunge pool; balcony; urban planting; loungers

In a sentence... A contemporary and highly stylised vision of urban living.

2 By dividing the space with different levels (here the steps down to the pool), designer Sarah Eberle has actually made the space feel bigger. She has also given this area a real sense of detail by adding mosaic tiles – this level of detail would be overly fussing throughout the whole garden space, but used specifically in this area of the pool it makes for a great addition to the materials on display.

3 Dense mixed planting on one side of the garden offers privacy and screening – vital commodities in an urban environment, where secluded personal space is so rare. A range of Mediterranean-type plants has been used here to thrive in the Monaco climate.

4 Maximising the use of space continues with the addition of a cantilevered balcony, emanating from the building, planted with lavender. The effect is to create a highly scented and private seating area.

5 Contemporary furniture is a must-have for such a space – the almost-floating soft mauve loungers add to the over-riding notion that this garden is one to relax and unwind in. When choosing such furniture, ensure that it matches – both tonally and stylistically – the surrounding architecture of the space.

Look around any city or town and you will often see little 'pockets' of spaces – land that developers forgot, that has slipped by without anyone really noticing. Such a premise has inspired many a designer, and often with fantastic results. In urban spaces, every centimetre counts. Just such a space featured in the 2009 RHS Chelsea Flower Show: Kate Gould's 'Eco Chic' was a subtle blend of environmental awareness with stylish design. Gardeners are increasingly wanting their space (whether rural or urban) to be stylish yet functional, contemporary yet environmentally considerate, useful yet attractive, and such design ideas found in this small area can help you realise your dreams in your own garden.

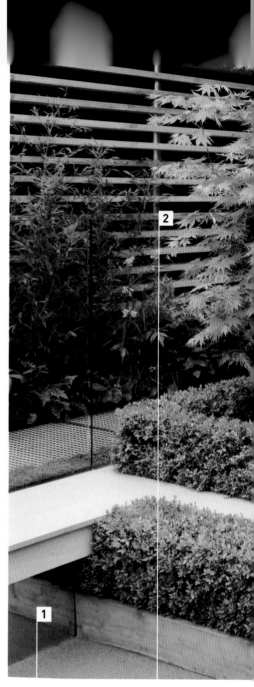

Balancing chic, contemporary design with recycled or reclaimed materials can often be a challenge – by their very nature they are not usual bedfellows. But in this garden, the designer managed to achieve a great harmony. The premise of the design had 'a pronounced eco edge' to it, by using discarded elements often left behind by builders and contractors. It was assumed that this garden was overlooked by surrounding buildings (often a reality in an urban environment) so planting was shade tolerant and continued up the wall to help reduce the visual impact of man-made materials. There really was a plethora of ideas in this space that can be taken to any garden, in any location – the fact that it was so convincing as a small, urban garden added to its appeal.

OTHER CONSIDERATIONS TO NOTE:

- the hard landscaping is permeable, so as to make use of every available drop of rain that might enter the space, as well as capturing and reusing 'grey water' from the adjacent buildings;
- the balance of materials is significant: the designer reused scaffold poles and boards, as well as introduced industrial materials such as expanded mesh walkways and glass panel screens;
- a water feature runs partially down the back wall, giving visual interest and movement, as well as helping block out surrounding noise;
- the visitor has a defined access point into the space (following a predetermined route often allows the designer to maximise all available space) and, in addition, level changes make the space feel much bigger;
- a 'living' wall softens the whole back wall and gives visual interest throughout the year; walls like these are becoming increasingly popular in show gardens and will soon become more so in domestic schemes.

1 Recessed, mirror-polished, stainless steel panels reflect available light and give a sense of depth to the space – just what you want in a tiny urban garden. This is typical of the ingenious little tricks that have been used so cleverly in this space.

2 Scaffold boards and poles have been thoroughly cleaned to emphasise the 'chic' look and make the best use of available materials. As a sensible precaution, a hardwood top board protects the softwood below.

DESIGNER Kate Gould

CONTRACTOR The Garden Builders

AWARD Gold; Best Urban Garden

CATEGORY Urban Garden, 2009

SPONSOR Helios

KEY WORDS stylish; urban space; angular; mixture of textures; 'living' wall; recycled materials

IN A SENTENCE... A great example of what you can achieve in any space by considering material selection, changing levels and planting combinations.

3 A beautifully shaped *Acer palmatum* brings colour and a soft texture to this 'hard' space and makes a central focal point. Planting has been considered carefully here. On the assumption that there are buildings on all sides, the chosen plants are shade tolerant, don't mind some sporadic damp or drought conditions and are generally considered pretty tough.

4 Permeable paving has been used to allow water to pass through and so make best use of all available water; any excess is captured and reused. Note also the physical fact that the visitor has to step down onto the paving, thereby giving the illusion of extra space.

5 'Living' walls are an ongoing trend in show gardens. There is still some work to be done by the industry to see how long such plantings can survive, and how much irrigation/maintenance they need, but their concept is to be welcomed. The main advantage of living walls is that they provide plenty of softness without taking up precious floor space. With the correct plant selection and establishment, their role should become increasingly significant in bringing greenery to cities everywhere.

6 A bench has been cantilevered to maintain an air gap beneath. Such seating is paramount to getting the most out of any outdoor space.

WATER

By working with many of the world's most ingenious water specialists, Chelsea designers have produced some truly memorable creations.

Of all elements that can be incorporated into a garden design, it is perhaps water that tests most gardeners. No such worries concern the designers at Chelsea, however, where the role and application of water has come on in leaps and bounds. The range of water effects will open your eyes to just what is possible, but the challenge can be to choose the most appropriate for your garden.

Over the years, all manner of water features have been on display at Chelsea – from natural-looking ponds, through long formal rills, to water apparently running uphill. Some creations are true 'statement' pieces, where shock and awe are the intention; others add a softer tone. Shapes and sizes abound, with raised troughs looking as good as stepped ponds; natural cascades comparing favourably with fountains and jets; simple urns with a trickle of water adding as much to a scheme as an infinity-edge swimming pool.

For many garden schemes the inclusion of a water feature is an integral part of the design: whether on the ground plan or vertical, without water the space would fail to work. It is perhaps in these schemes, where water plays as crucial a role as a tree or patio, that you can start to consider why water gardening in your private garden needs care and attention. Considering many different issues will help you focus your requirements.

Not only do the Chelsea gardens show you big or small, modern or traditional, simple or complicated water gardening, but they also provide you with tricks of the trade. Take the colour black, for example. Not a natural water colour, yet 'black' ponds nearly always feature. There are two main ways of creating the effect: by lining the pond structure with a taut black plastic, or by painting the sides and bottom black; or, for a short-term effect, dye is added to the water to make it black. Whichever way is chosen, an illusion of depth is created. Many of the water features may be just 30cm (12in) deep,

but by making them black the viewer is tricked into thinking they are something bigger.

Reflection is also a key factor for many designers: flat calm water often creates a different atmosphere in the space, reflecting light, clouds, sun, trees and so on. Other conceits employed, which can be easily mirrored in a domestic setting, include: tying in (or contrasting) the colour of the pool or pond with paving, fencing or planting; lighting certain parts of the water body (such as a fountain or rill) to extend its visual appeal into the evening; and adding misting machines that can lend an air of mystery and the fantastical to a creation.

MAKING WATER WORK

Ponds and water features range from rain-fed seasonal ponds, through off-the-shelf water features to large-scale pools or ponds or formal water channels such as rills. Whatever you desire, make sure you know how the effect will work in your garden, and research water gardening in detail. Look at magazines, books or open gardens for inspiration. If in any doubt, you can consult your local pond or water specialist. Consider also the need for any pumping or electricity: remember that only qualified electricians can bring an electricity supply into your garden.

FIRST STEPS TO WATER GARDENING

Including water in your home garden can be a big decision, so consider your responses to some of these necessary questions:

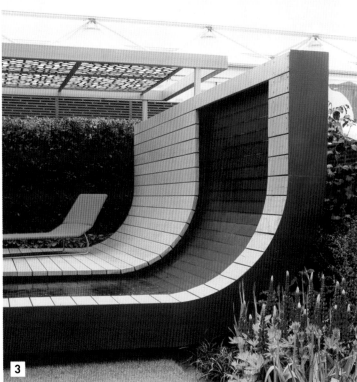

- Why do you want water?
- What role is it playing and what is it adding to your space?
- Do you want something that will block out noise, or is it more a visual requirement, such as adding movement?
- Should the water be flat or uneven?
- Is the water for interacting with (getting into it and getting wet) or is it something that you would prefer to view from a certain distance?
- Is safety an issue (especially with younger children or pets)?
- How will wildlife benefit from including a water garden in your scheme?
- Does the feature need electricity to make it work (pump and lighting, for example)?
- How much maintenance will it require each year to make it look as good as intended?
- Are you wanting a small, floor-mounted water feature bought from a local shop or does your idea require building works or planning regulations?

- Do you need a deep structure, or can you get away with a much more shallow effect?
- Will you need specialist advice to make your desire become a reality?

Clearly, the answers to these questions aren't always going to be straightforward, but if you can't answer them yet you may need more consideration time. The larger the water feature, the less forgiving the end result will be if you have not thought the plan through.

Water really can bring a new dimension to any garden, be it large or small, rural or urban. But careful siting, consideration of how the effect will be created and the need for ongoing maintenance, make water features less of an impulse buy than some might consider. There is a style of water gardening to suit all tastes and a wide range of budgets, so do not hurry your decision. However, after exploring the range of designs over the next few pages, your imagination is the one thing the water feature in your garden never need lack.

1 Juxtaposing two different styles of water feature into a space can be a clever design technique. For instance, here a scalloped rill leads into the straight lines of a reflective pool, focusing and directing not only your eye, but also the passage of water.

2 Small, organic-shaped self-contained pools, here symbolising rock pools along the Cornish coast, reflect the sky and visually continue the watery theme to the large pool beyond.

3 As it flows down the inside of this curved wall, the water gives a sense of movement and shine to the black timber. It then levels out to form a shallow lap pool.

Simple and effective water

When most people think of including water in their home garden, an image of a small, natural-looking pond or off-the-shelf water feature is conjured up. However, these features never really produce the often-required need for reflection, views or drama. Introducing still water into a garden can be a daunting task, but with confidence and an eye for detail it can be dramatic and significant.

Done really well it can set the whole tone of the outside space. The materials and shape can reflect any style of design, but consideration must also be given to its scale, maintenance requirements, topographical demands, the safety for garden users and its possible attraction to household pets. Once these are answered, flat water can then become an integral part of a great garden design.

1

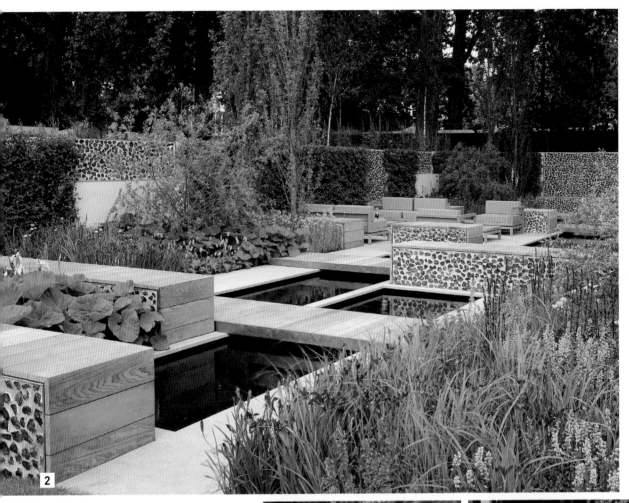

2

STILL WATERS SOMETIMES RUN DEEP

Even though some of these creations are for show gardens, their principles can easily be applied to a home garden.

1 This expanse of seemingly bottomless water acts like a blank sheet dividing lawn from building. Note the ingenious square shafts where the water falls over the edge and down into the void below – a great piece of design.

2 Using water to complement other materials is a clever trick: here, simple rectangles of still water continue the linear grid of this space, softened by dense planting on the outside edges. Deck walkways seemingly hover above the water at right angles.

3 Water acts like a sheen over these beautiful sculptures, and in so doing shows how it can enhance another garden feature.

4 This long thin mini-canal directs the visitor's eye to the orangery at the far end – a traditional design technique in formal and often grand gardens.

3

4

DEFINED ROLE

Water can often be used successfully in a complementary, low-key way; it doesn't always have to be the main focus of a design.

1 The blue glass sculpture is the centre of attention here, while the water at its base plays second fiddle but helps 'anchor' the sculpture into the scene.

2 Movement, texture and simplicity are all entwined in this creation; there is writing beneath the water's surface, while the step down reinforces the sense of movement.

3 This mirror-polished steel sculptural form, surrounded by lush, green ferns, makes a huge statement of high-quality design in this garden's cool corner.

4 A holed-out stone provides a perfect balance to the informal planting and rustic fence, and is easily replicated in a home garden. Such simplicity can be highly effective.

5 Rusting steel troughs seem to slice through the raised tree canopy above and frothy planting below. Their successful positioning exemplifies how important it is to consider how any container will sit within its surroundings.

6 The subtle addition of water hawthorn (*Aponogeton distachyos*) in this over-sized container brings colour to the flat surface, and gives interest to the overall effect.

1

2

EXPERT TIP
Andrew Ewing Edging water

❝ The use of an appropriate material around your water feature can substantially enhance its overall design and effect. For a minimal edging, say, between grass and water, stainless steel set upright produces a crisp line and can allow the water height to be almost level with the grass. Otherwise stone is a great edging material, whether cut clean in a modern style or left more naturalistic and jagged. When using stone it always helps to have an overhang at the side of the pool, to create an elegant line and to help conceal any pond lining. Other materials can of course be used, but they raise very real and practical concerns of load bearing (that is, how much weight that material can take when stood on) and fixing (if there is an overhang over the water, how do you ensure that standing on the overhang won't make the visitor topple into the water). Consider also wildlife needs, in terms of how amphibians may enter or exit the water, and also the role and requirements of aquatic and marginal planting if desired. Such planting can 'soften' the edge of a water feature, directing attention onto the plants and water itself. ❞

ACHIEVING A NATURAL FEEL

Informal planting, irregular edges and rustic materials can combine to create a strong effect.

1 This pond adds to the overall feel of a naturally inspired garden by looking as if it has been here for many years, The effect is made all the more convincing by marginal planting, rocks and plenty of algae.

2 By using different pebbles and boulders, along with water-wise planting, the water here is taking a natural course.

3 Water flows through a main pond, flanked by shallow overflow pools, in this recreation of a cottage-style garden. The materials and design were chosen to cope with flash flooding and sporadic heavy rainfall.

4 Chelsea pensioners add to this quintessentially British scene of a derelict fence tumbling into an informal water area. Dressed in their famous red coats, the pensioners are an intrinsic part of the show, which is held at the grounds of the Royal Hospital Chelsea.

[above] Having a defined, visible edge to a body of water is a sensible precaution to take, and much can be made of it in terms of material choice and its shape.

[right] A more naturalistic approach to edging a pond here uses *Sarracenia* arising out of 'black' water, with a timber deck beyond. Note the *Sarracenia* would not be hardy in cool-temperate regions.

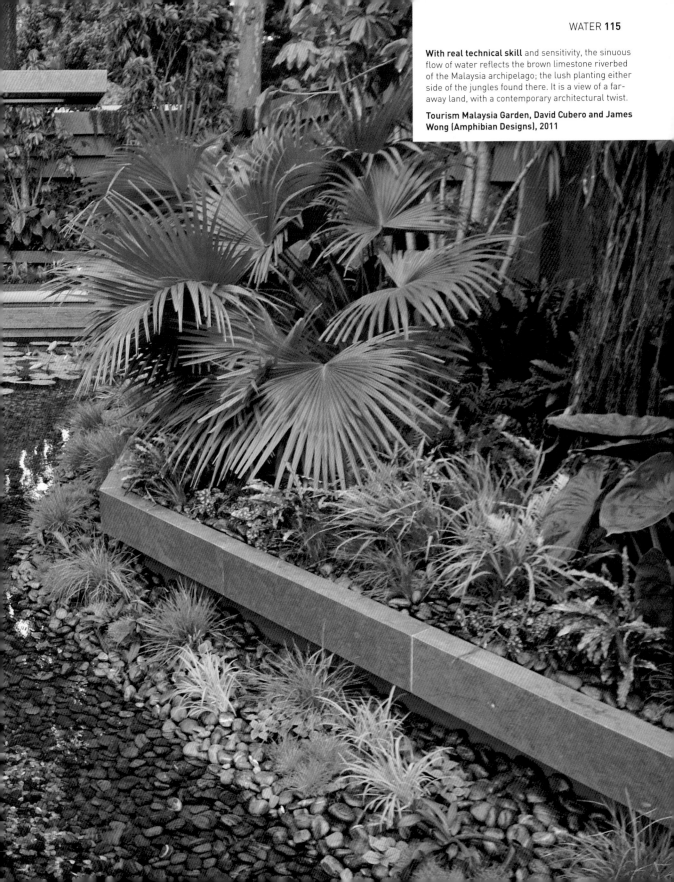

With real technical skill and sensitivity, the sinuous flow of water reflects the brown limestone riverbed of the Malaysia archipelago; the lush planting either side of the jungles found there. It is a view of a far-away land, with a contemporary architectural twist.

Tourism Malaysia Garden, David Cubero and James Wong (Amphibian Designs), 2011

Movement in all shapes and sizes

Gardeners and designers often want water features to be visually useful as well as dynamic and interesting. One way of contributing to such a goal is to make the water move – whether a slow trickle or full-on jet. Either way, moving water can not only look incredibly attractive and dramatic – no matter what the style – but it can also ensure oxygen is introduced to the water, which in turns helps reduce stagnation. If creating a feature with moving water, however, beware that substantial disturbance may upset wildlife and some plants, so consider the type of motion needed for the effect desired. Also understand how the movement is to be created (pump? gravity?) and if it will require additional technical knowledge. Water can be a difficult material to make work well, so research and predict what problems may arise before getting the spade out and making your dream creation.

4

6

7

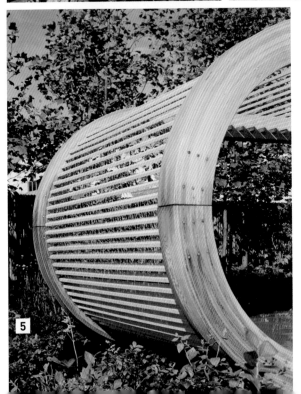

5

FORM AND STYLE FOR ANY GARDEN

Making water move can be achieved in myriad ways, from shoots or waterfalls to containers or jets.

1 This simple linear feature lets the water fall into a trough below, and at night it is accentuated by the addition of a bright white-red light.

2 A water jet 'leaping' over the planting onto the wall beyond brings a sense of the unexpected to a small urban space. Such an element of surprise can be a real novelty in a garden.

3 Misting machines can be used to add an air of mystery or drama to water, but the context and the surrounding materials are crucial to make sure the rising mist looks convincing.

4 This glass sculpture, by light sculptor Iestyn Davies, features oil and air, swirling and mixing around to great effect; colour-changing LED lights accentuate the drama at night.

5 On this back 'wall', water drips from one slat to another, accentuating the natural curve and using water to bring added movement. By merging structure, sculpture and water feature all into one, the designer has created a work of art in itself.

6 Waterfalls, when done well, can be a great way to hide an unsightly wall, unwanted view or block out noise. As here, ensure the drop of each water layer is well positioned and physically relates to those above or below.

7 This swirling vortex is an interesting detail within a much larger expanse of otherwise still water.

1

3

2

JETS FOR VERTICAL FORM

By making water rise vertically, in the form of a spray or jet, movement and energy can be introduced into a design.

1 This simple spray of water can be included in any domestic water feature; ensure surrounding planting is moisture-tolerant as wind can blow water in different directions.

2 Low 'bubbles' help move the body of water over the raised plinth edge to the basin below. Blending such simplicity with highly skilled construction techniques can be quite challenging, but the end result, as here, is well worth it.

3 Spiralling glass pebbles around the outside of the feature accentuate the strong thick jet. Their placement adds movement, and the white froth of the water creates a sense of energy.

4 The combination of square pool, vertical jet, double layer box hedge and wide steps makes for a simply stunning formal scheme that is both refined and proportionally exact.

[right] These simple cubes of water with their flat surfaces reflect the sky and light from above, and contrast in tone and texture with the plants around them.

[far right] A great sculptured white 'ball' here seems to be sending out ripples of water from its epicentre as well as subtly mirroring the sky and trees.

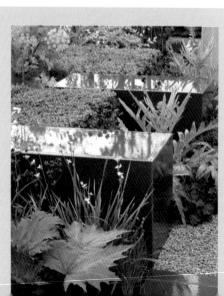

EXPERT TIP
Andrew Ewing Reflections

❝ The basic principle of creating reflections is to use a dark material as a liner for the pool. If you envisage a puddle on black Tarmac you can understand this; although the puddle may be only a couple of centimetres deep, it can create a perfect mirror image. The lining material in the pool is not important, but its colouring is. For a sharp reflection, the water needs to appear as still as possible, with no debris disturbing the surface. This can be a problem in small urban gardens (with leaves or pollen falling onto the

4

surface) but if you can plan the location of the water feature in the most open area of your plot, that is ideal. Ensuring the water feature is also built level is crucial, because the water surface will be unforgiving if there is even a slight camber. Remember, however, that even though reflections are amazing for many water features, on overcast and dull days the effect can be diminished, so be sure you choose the style and shape of your water feature correctly. Lighting can also be considered in tandem with the use of reflections: think about highlighting the feature to be mirrored in the water, not the water itself, so for example illuminate a tree that will be reflected in the water. The end result can be a really subtle but stunning way to link the night-time atmosphere of planting with the water in your garden. '

DROPS FOR DRAMA

A sheer drop or a more subtle 'stepped' effect can each set the overall tone of a water feature to great effect.

1 This sheer wall is a magnificent creation – especially as the reclining incline is subtle, offset beautifully by the surrounding yew hedge, and simple gravel strip at its base; at night, the spotlights create even more drama.

2 A rusticated rock wall artfully mimics the sense of energy and movement one might expect with a natural waterfall. The placement of submerged lights adds to the feeling of water plunging into a deep pool below. The white allium flowerheads in the foreground are also well set off by the water.

3 Simple droplets of water fall from one slat to the next, helping create a semitransparent screen.

4 This 'wall' of water cascades from a thick metal top bar, to produce a moving, changeable and unusual feature.

5 Precision-perfect flat water, defined level changes and varying pace combine to sublime effect. Many elements (sculpture, water, planting, movement) were brought together in this scheme, which sought to represent the flow of New Zealand water from mountain streams down to the sea.

5

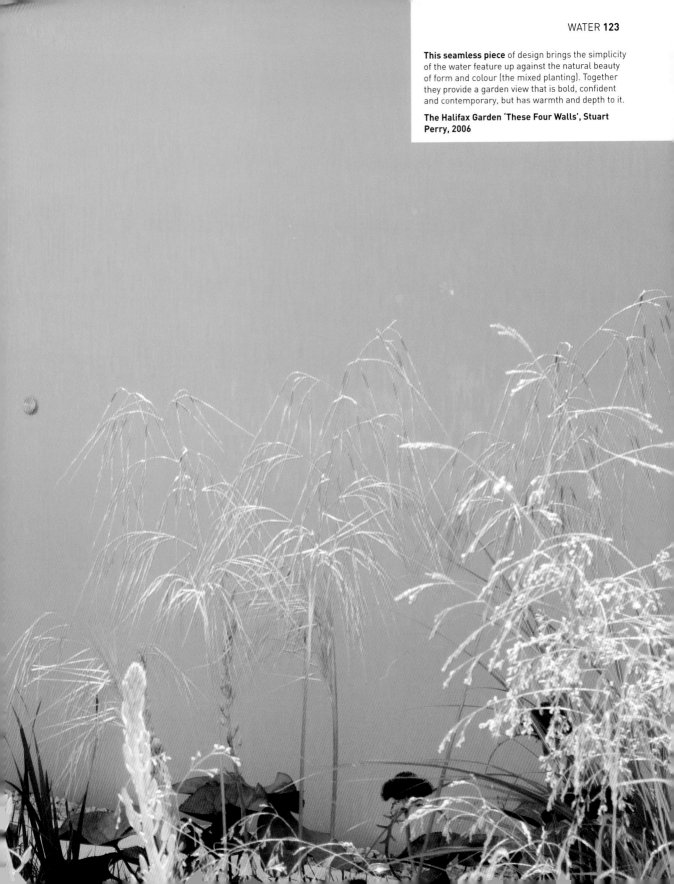

This seamless piece of design brings the simplicity of the water feature up against the natural beauty of form and colour (the mixed planting). Together they provide a garden view that is bold, confident and contemporary, but has warmth and depth to it.

The Halifax Garden 'These Four Walls', Stuart Perry, 2006

FOCUSING WATER'S DIRECTION

There are many ways in which water can be channelled, and these can vary from bold statements to simple effects.

1 This stainless steel water arc provides an entrance to the garden, while the swirling mosaic (created by Maggy Howarth) continues the aquatic theme.

2 A contemporary glass sculpture channels the movement of water in a specific direction. Speed of flow and cleanliness of water are essential in helping this design succeed.

3 Water from a slot in the wall drops into the basin below. Such a simple detail could be introduced to enliven the corner of a wall in any home garden.

4 A small water chute cleverly mirrors the size of the wooden cubes, while water from its outflow forms random paths down the steps.

5 The beauty of this design is the pared down collection of materials: stone, water, spout and planting (grasses and hedging). For such a composition to succeed it must be designed with restraint and consideration, taking great attention to detail and determination to only use the very best products available.

6 Three lacquered-steel bespoke water features project out of this wall – their shape was inspired by an arum lily.

5

6

THE DAILY TELEGRAPH GARDEN

Having the confidence to fill much of your allocated space at the RHS Chelsea Flower Show with water requires real conviction. In this garden, Arabella Lennox-Boyd showed how water can play equal fiddle to inanimate objects, such as stones or paving, and to ever-changing subjects such as plants and trees. Her pared-down space used quality materials rather than garden-gizmos to show what can be achieved when Japanese design principles are combined with English planting.

Often at Chelsea, gardens are created on the assumption that what is on display would actually make up only part of a larger garden, if it were ever to enter 'the real world'. With this in mind, it is easy to start to appreciate this design more and more. A large rectangle of water takes up nearly three-quarters of the space, yet the designer's intention to 'simply provide delight and to create an atmosphere of peace and relaxation' cannot be refuted.

WHY THIS GARDEN WORKS SO WELL:

- the water area is crossed by two ribbons of differing materials – one of waterlily *Nymphaea alba* and the other of a Burlington-slate path;
- the sinuous lines of these ribbons converge and retreat, so they are visually balanced by two large slate rocks;
- the visitor's eye is then lifted to the planting: along one edge a clipped tiered yew hedge, and then at the end is an area of dense planting consisting of greens, whites, beige/yellows and textured bark and stems;
- the mirror-like qualities of the water reflect nearby and far-off views;
- the detailing, whether slate mulch surrounding the water or the stones that emerge from it, is pin sharp and very clean;
- a hidden mirror behind the bamboo stems at the far end gives extra depth and light to the whole space.

So what about home gardens? This design tells you everything you need to know about water: why levels are so important; how to use materials that will visually link across a scheme; and the reflective quality that only water can bring and how best to use it. It also gives neat ideas: that of balancing dense planting (a mass) with the air above the water (a void); of simple-to-achieve lines (the water's edge, yew hedge and so on) that hold the space and take the garden visitor from one space to another; and of harmonious planting in terms of flower and leaf colour.

And don't forget the mirror behind the bamboo – a great trick that anyone can achieve, as long as you remember to hide the mirror's edges with dense planting so you can't see where the mirror starts and ends.

DESIGNER Arabella Lennox-Boyd

CONTRACTOR Crocus.co.uk

AWARD Gold

CATEGORY Show Garden, 2008

SPONSOR *The Daily Telegraph*

KEY WORDS water; path; green-and-white planting; bamboo stems; reflection; waterlilies

IN A SENTENCE... A calming balancing act between planting, water and stone.

1 *Pterocarya fraxinifolia* – a vigorous, spreading tree that likes to grow in deep, fertile, moist but well-drained soil – visually offsets the flat calm water and gives height to the space. Its ovate, glossy green leaves contrast nicely with the slender form of the neighbouring *Phyllostachys* bamboo.

2 *Gunnera manicata*, a large-leaved, waterside-loving plant, creates a strong focal point at the end of the garden, contrasting in both texture and shape with the yew hedge to the right, and sleek paving below.

3 This slate path brings movement and curves to the rectangular water area, which it divides. The sweep of the path is cleverly mirrored by sinuous plantings of white waterlily – an ingenious way of using different materials while retaining a consistent design effect.

4 Tall rocks within a water feature should be considered in terms of how and where most visitors will view the design. This will provoke the strongest 'wow' factor.

5 The expanse of water contributes greatly to the success of this garden, as do the subsequent reflections that are created not only of the surrounding trees of *Platanus* x *hispanica* or the focal-point bamboos, but also of the clouds and pockets of white sky.

6 Waterlilies *Nymphaea alba*, planted in two opposing curves, form part of the floral splendour of this garden, which comes from the restrained palette of plants used and their flower colour – purely white and yellow.

To make water a truly integral part of a garden design, it must be considered from the very outset. Whether a contemporary reflective pool or a more formal pond, the use of water can add to the atmosphere and visual appearance of any outdoor space. It can bring something quite different from planting or hard materials; reflection, a changing light palette and movement add to a garden's dynamic elements. It can also make a visitor slow down, providing an area for contemplation and consideration.

It is perhaps these last attributes that work so well and support designer Roger Platts' inclusion of a circular pool in this space. It is both understated and low key, yet vital and essential to the overall design. The simple shape is accentuated by the stone edging, echoed by the mounded hedges, and mirrored again in the crescent timber beams of the barn. The design is quintessentially, unapologetically British – and all the better for it. Placement of a body of water in a garden can be difficult at home, but Roger's deceptively simple approach of using a circular shape, mirrored by lots of rounded forms elsewhere in the space, gives an inspiring end result for people to try at home. The less clever you try to be with water, often the better the result.

INCLUDING WATER IN A GARDEN:

- simplicity is key – fast-moving water features can be complicated to build and create an unrelaxing atmosphere yet a calm body of water is far more tranquil;
- get value for your water feature, reflecting surrounding plants or the overhead sky – tucking it away under foliage can mean it goes unnoticed;
- don't place water bodies too near trees or dense planting, as leaves can fall into the pond during winter and affect the quality of the water;
- the shape of a water feature needs to be in harmony with the garden's overall design – straight lines could look out of context in a space full of curves;
- ponds and pools are havens for wildlife, consider ramps or a collection of stones so animals such as frogs can get into and out of the water;
- fish can be kept in sufficiently-sized ponds, but remember they are 'predators' so normally reduce the diversity of wildlife.

1 The simple stone edging has rounded sides which give it a quality feel and reinforce the over-riding 'circular' design ethos that runs throughout this garden – even with such a seemingly small detail as this, a designer can continue a design concept to create a cohesive space.

DESIGNER Roger Platts

CONTRACTOR Roger Platts & N.R. Jupp

AWARD Gold

CATEGORY Show Garden, 2010

SPONSOR M&G Investments

KEY WORDS water; pool; calm; reflection; English style; muted colour; classical

IN A SENTENCE... A beautifully-executed design that brings the best of British garden style, using water as a focal point.

2 Flat, calm water is a great way of slowing down a visitor to a garden and creating a relaxing and tranquil environment. The surface reflects the sky and surrounding light to add atmosphere to the space.

3 Mounded hummocks of *Buxus* (box) bring greenery and texture around the pool and continue the circular theme echoed in the rest of the design.

4 Flower colour has been kept intentionally muted, with green leaves, white flowers and the 'borrowed' views of trees beyond adding to the calm nature of this space and a feeling of enclosure and security.

5 This beautifully-crafted timber loggia continues the English feel in this garden and shows how useable this area is – it is easy to imagine the enjoyment a visitor could have sitting in this outside 'room', looking over the surrounding planting and tranquil pool.

MATERIALS

Whether a brand-new material
or an older material used in
a contemporary and different
way, the endless creativity
on display at Chelsea is utterly
breathtaking.

One thing that Chelsea designers really enjoy is being able to experiment with new materials. It gives these creative people the opportunity to try out some new techniques or products that their working life may not afford them. No real clients, no real restrictions; no real issues of taste and no practical problems of longevity or weather – this show lets them break rules and push tried-and-tested boundaries.

Garden and landscape designers are often reputed to have quite a lonely existence in their working lives. Of course, they see their clients and suppliers, but much of the time is spent on their own, devising designs, creating planting plans and sourcing products. Yet by nature most are creative, design-aware people who enjoy the stimulation of working with others and challenging artisans – from sculptors to builders, carpenters to quarrymen – to transform their ideas into reality. The ever-expanding exchange of information and ideas from architects, interior designers, sculptors and product designers is increasingly leading to a healthy development of visual and conceptual exploration. Sharing ideas, learning from other trades and researching other professions all feed an appetite for new concepts. RHS Chelsea Flower Show is, in a way, the end of that process for many designers as it is a forum where they can showcase the results of this development process. But for the gardening public, it may be just the start.

So what type of materials are being shown at Chelsea? In short, any. During recent years, more glass has been used outside, as a direct result of advancements in specification and manufacturing. Whether as screens or balustrades, tables or water sculptures, glass can be an expensive yet splendid addition to a show garden. So too can metal – from stainless steel planters to rusting steel, the diversity of finishes to, and types of, metal can provide endless opportunity for designers. The form in which metal has often been included varies from the rustic to the contemporary, low-key to the overt, bespoke to off-the-shelf items. Perspex, normally attributed to indoor products, has also been used in some show gardens in recent years, as developments in its formation – plus the realisation that it can bring colour and a variety of shapes to a garden – have been welcomed by those wanting a statement feature. As well as these man-made materials, long-appreciated timber never fails to whet designer's appetites, either in fantastic sculptural additions (see case study, p150) or in much smaller interventions of seating or tables.

Much of what is seen at Chelsea can trigger the reaction 'I want one of those' – even by the most restrained of gardeners. However what is on display in a show garden may be completely new to the garden world, so its longevity, its ability to cope with years of changeable weather conditions, and its actual structural rigidity are not necessarily proven. It may be a designer's chance to try out a technique or concept as yet unseen – something that may look visually stunning but actually needs further refinement. This doesn't mean that you shouldn't get excited when you see a material used in a completely different way, but it may be best to temper your enthusiasm by considering just how well that material would work in a real, 365-days-a-year garden.

The upshot of all this design novelty is often to be seen in the garden centres and DIY shops a few years later. Just like the catwalk of the fashion world, techniques and products on

1

1 Using materials from unexpected sources can be personally rewarding and environmentally friendly. Here the designer has included offcuts of wood – by-products from the timber industry – to create a decorative and textured wall. The variation in colour and the way that the wood has been laid at varying indentations make for a great effect.

2 Experimenting with new materials is essential for Chelsea designers. Here, a technique to reduce the carbon footprint of concrete manufacturing has been applied to these wall adornments.

3 Drama can be created using a range of clever design principles. Here the combination of three primary materials – steel, stone and timber – contrast yet complement each other.

4 The 'magic' of different materials can be exploited by their application as much as by their inherent form. The different lines – here of a bench and retaining wall, softened by colourful planting – make for a visual treat.

display at Chelsea sometimes end up (sometimes pared down) in the home environment. Consider the fire pit, for example: a simple device, either dug into the ground or standing proud (similar to a mini-barbecue) that allows you to burn wood in your garden, in a safe and attractive way. Seen at Chelsea in different guises over the years, it is now a common item among some of the more contemporary product lines in fashionable garden-related shops.

Fortunately, the net result for all garden consumers is an expansion of choice and range of styles, whether these act as an aesthetic stimulation that sparks an interest in the viewer, or a few years later they result in a product that has been developed for the mass market. For some visitors, Chelsea show gardens provide the encouragement to recreate the same designs at home; for others, they supply the source for an appropriate artisan or manufacturer to fulfil their immediate needs. What is certain is that the material magic of Chelsea show gardens will continue to challenge and stimulate the creative minds of designers and gardeners alike.

Metal in many guises

The advent of more refined manufacturing techniques, plus the ever-expanding thirst of designers for novelty, have brought a host of new ideas on how to use different metals in a garden setting at the RHS Chelsea Flower Show. From planters to dividing screens, planting edges to garden sculptures, the practical and visual appeal of metal is integral to many show gardens. One such example has been the popular use of gabions (metal cages filled with stone, soil or any other material) that derive from the civil engineering industry, and are intended to retain landform behind. Their application in show gardens has brought a whole new suite of ideas fresh from designers.

But it is perhaps the variety of end results that makes using metal so interesting. Whether it is stainless steel or galvanised, brushed or polished, steel especially has brought new opportunities for designers both as the primary material on show and in a supporting role. And, as is often the case with Chelsea ideas, similar ideas and styles are now percolating through the supply chain into garden centres, DIY stores or through online shops.

1

2

3

ANY SHAPE WILL DO

From gabions to sculpture, planters to water features, metal engineering can be introduced in a range of ways.

1 This repetitively shaped planter is a great addition to any wall or small space, providing vertical interest to a garden. Each individual unit – here growing pansies – gives just enough planting depth for a seasonal display.

2 A simple cylindrical design evokes a futuristic feel in this space. The smooth metallic surface complements beautifully the weeping habit of this cactus.

3 Soda-blasted aluminium 'thought bubbles' have been designed to link with the sponsor's message. Their inclusion nicely balances the green wall behind, contrasting in both form and colour with the foreground planting and clean linear steps.

4 Where gabions are used in a garden setting, the engineering requirement may be reduced, while the aesthetic benefit they bring is truly maximised.

5 By combining water and steel a dramatic impression can be created in a garden, as can be seen here, where water is flowing down the sides of these sculptural features.

4

5

This garden combines a feeling of spaciousness with modernity, by its use of a reinforced glass flooring overlaid on flowing water. Using your outside space in imaginative ways is becoming increasingly popular where open space is limited.

The Witan Wisdom Garden, Nicholas Dexter, 2009

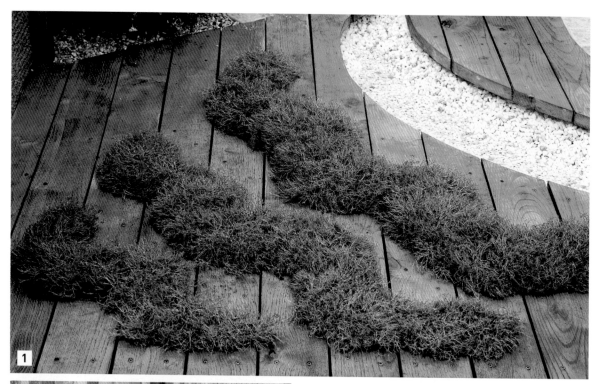

Just add timber

Wood is probably the most versatile of garden materials. Not only does it have a huge emotional attraction for many gardeners (who doesn't love to stand against a mighty oak or stroke an unusual bark?), but it can also be made into seats, fences, steps, structures, screens or surfaces. Timber is timeless and can be used to great effect – in a modern or traditional, formal or naturalistic way. Its finishes too are endless, with stains, paints, effects and quality providing huge possibilities, as demonstrated so successfully by designers in the RHS Chelsea Flower Show gardens. There, the ability of craftspeople to sculpt and transform a piece of wood from a designer's concept into an actual reality can be fully appreciated. And it is this combining of skills – designer vision with technical ability – that is at the heart of so many gardening successes throughout the world.

3

4

TIMBER IN DIFFERENT GUISES

Working with timber can be enjoyable in any garden, whether you are an enthusiastic amateur or skilled carpenter.

1 To break up the linear effect of this decking, chamomile has been planted across the timber lines. The 'squiggle' effect makes for a really interesting contrast, allowing planting and wood to balance each other.

2 First-grade Western red cedar has been used in this scheme. It is a timber full of natural resins which make it highly durable – and not necessary to stain. As the wood naturally weathers, it will become a more silver colour. The cantilevered bench makes good use of space.

3 Seemingly random cubes of oak rise at different heights from the black water below, acting as a flight of steps. The aquatic and marginal planting softens the overall effect, and the result is a great example of material combination.

4 Decking is an ever-popular flooring material for both professional and home gardeners, but the addition of different materials – such as the steel mesh here – can make the result more visually exciting.

5 To partition this space, the designer placed the perforated timber 'walls' at a slight diagonal across the garden. The silver-grey paint references the colour used on many buildings in the Swedish countryside (linking to the design theme).

5

Full on colour

While well-planned planting selections can bring foliage and floral colour to most gardens, inanimate objects can really help add a blast of much-needed vibrancy. Containers or planters can be used to provide a strong block of colour, while paving can be designed so there is a consistent 'flow' of tonal texture in a space. More dramatic additions can be verging on the sculptural, with mosaics or surface treatments bringing a whole

new range of hues and shades to an otherwise ordinary garden. Before using colour so boldly, however, there are two important considerations: make sure you really like the colours you are including (as the novelty value can soon wear off); and remember that strong vivid colours can look somewhat ungainly or out-of-place under overcast grey skies. Once you have resolved these issues, colour can be welcomed with great enthusiasm.

SPECTRUM OF CHOICE

A host of materials from glass to stone, metal to timber can be introduced to expand the colour range in a garden.

1 This dramatic container creates a definite focal point – the swirling mosaic design on the outside is continued within, in the form of a sculptural plant. Note how the colours are carried on at ground level with red and yellow bedding plants.

2 The detail and intricacy of a design such as this mosaic path is not for the faint hearted, and must be undertaken by a skilled artisan for best effect.

3 Coloured glass panes reflect the changing light on a sunny day, or add a visual boost to more overcast times. The planting is low allergen (ideal for hayfever sufferers), and links to some of the colour tones from the glass itself.

4 Colours, textures, shapes and styles abound in this view, from the traditional deckchairs on the roof of the garden room to the stone-filled gabions, with masses of dense and colourful planting in the foreground. This accumulation of colour makes for a bold and flamboyant effect.

Bringing the space alive

Screens, walls, fences and hedges are popular design elements used in all types of gardens (see also pp32–7). Their use can be practical (to define a certain area of planting or give climatic protection) or it can be physical (to make a space feel bigger or a certain area more intimate). Yet the material that they are constructed from can help set the whole tone of the garden. The colour can inject excitement or calm; the texture can be rough, smooth, metallic or matt; the size can be proportionate, overdominant or undersized; and the material itself can clash or complement. Whatever materials or techniques you use for delineating your garden, ensure that they can withstand the vagaries of the weather, can be maintained to the standard required, and will mature and develop as intended.

DIVIDING SPACE

A range of techniques can be adopted to make a space feel bigger.

1 Orange Perspex screens help give depth and interest to this space. Note how the colour of the screens links to the orange-red tulips, while the burgundy-leaved *Dahlia* adds a darker tone.

2 Undulating grass paths in this scheme create movement and flow, and help trick the visitor's eye into thinking the space is bigger than it is. Smooth painted render on the side walls enhance the effect.

3 An image of botanist, scientist and explorer Carl Linnaeus has been imprinted on a vertical, laser-cut sheet of steel in this garden so he seemingly overlooks the space. The screen also breaks up the view of the white-flowering foxgloves and hedge beyond.

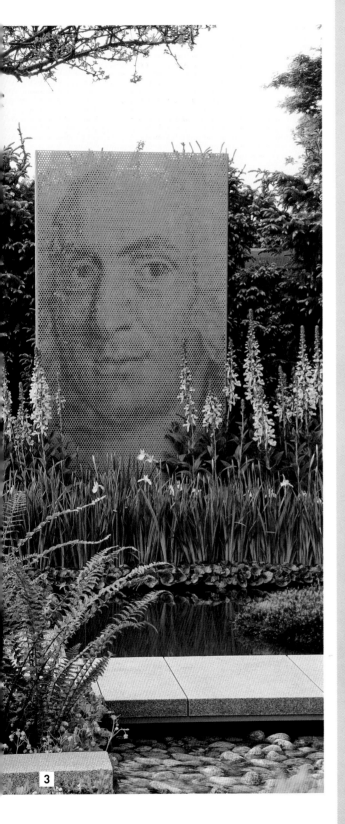

EXPERT TIP

Andy Sturgeon Using glass

❛Glass is useful in the garden for furniture, screens, balustrades and flooring but is quite a specialist material that often needs expert installation. Generally speaking it should be toughened for safety and should not have sharp corners at adult or child head height. Clear glass requires regular cleaning as it readily shows the dirt; opaque, coloured or patterned glass perhaps less so. Acrylic/Perspex/Plexiglass (it's all the same material) is lighter and less expensive than glass, making it a better choice for roof gardens and balconies, and for gardens where access is difficult. It is far more versatile, easier to cut, polish and glue and readily available in a wide range of colours and therefore suitable for anything from planters to water features and clever lighting features. Ultraviolet and impact-resistant acrylics are available but being quite flexible they are less able to take loads than glass, making them unsuitable for flooring or balustrades. Avoid abrasive cleaning products on acrylics.❜

While allowing light to filter in, these glass panels help divide this small space into a path on the left and a planting area to the right.

This 'outdoor office' envisions an enjoyable, useful working environment. It has areas for staff to work alone or have meetings; new materials are used (the planters are recycled plastic); and textured planting contrasts with the hard landscaping.

Rooftop Workplace of Tomorrow, Patricia Fox (Aralia Garden Design), 2012

1

Thinking outside the box

Some of the most innovative, aesthetic designs sometimes stem from combining materials that are not normally seen together. Putting rough with the smooth, the bright with the plain or the textured with the matt is fun but challenging. To mix materials skilfully you need an understanding of their similarities as well as their differences. Should you be contrasting form with texture, or practicality with visual drama? Can one material embellish another, or should both be equal partners? How can one material physically juxtapose another, especially when both materials may require different construction techniques? When done badly, some material combinations can look a mess; by looking tacky the final effect can unintentionally destroy the original thoughts behind them. When done well, on the other hand, they can be creative, stimulating and a fresh way of viewing materials.

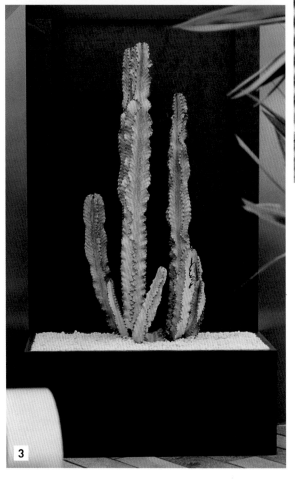

DIFFERENT MATERIALS, DIFFERENT IDEAS

Mixing materials takes skill and effort, but when done well the results can be really exciting.

1 These terracotta- and stone-filled gabions not only provide a sustainable response by using reclaimed or old materials, but also act as a low retaining wall to the planting behind. The additional benefit for insects to nest or house within the gaps is considerable.

2 Handcrafted zinc tanks feature throughout this garden, the still black water complementing the silver-grey of the zinc container (see case study, p78). Such simplicity in material juxtaposition can create sublime detailing.

3 These striking mature cacti look fabulous within the black planter, with a black wall behind creating a cool calm atmosphere. The white mulch also heightens the sense of modernity.

4 Designers are not allowed to include current models of cars in gardens, as this could be deemed advertising, but here a crushed car has been recycled to help form an outdoor table. Surrounded by clean, modern lines, the contrast of texture and colour is a great success.

5 The concept for this space was an outside gallery, displaying a private collection of photographs. The metallic side panels, framed photographs and rendered wall combine to strong effect.

When creating gardens, designers often discuss the need for a 'concept' or 'theme' – not an idea that is so restrictive that it stifles creativity, but rather a hook to hang a garden's design on. It should allow for ideas, for a story to be told, and to act as an anchor for planting and hard materials. In this garden, leading landscape architect Robert Myers has done just that – his theme of a 'coastal landscape' has been interpreted with a modern twist, using a consistent but relatively wide range of materials. The end result is a feeling of being by the coast but without the pastiche of how a garden near the sea would normally look.

The design has been pared down to the essential elements of a coastal landscape – water, timber, plants and rock. By considering each of these materials in their own right, and by adding the concept of 'surviving' (which links to the garden's sponsor), Robert's aim has been to transport people from the front of the space (representing a shore), along a journey through the space, ending at the outdoor seating area. This metaphorical journey of 'survival' is subtle, but once understood, helps you appreciate how he has created his garden. His choice of plants, and the hard landscaping materials, link across the visual appeal of the space, as well as enhancing the design concept.

COASTAL IDEAS TO TRY AT HOME:

- a coastal theme is a great way of bringing a cohesive feel to a garden, because planting, hard materials and buildings (or decoration) can be visually tied together;
- material choice is vitally important when you do have a specific theme, ensure the planting, metals, timber and stone 'tie in' to the overall scheme;
- Robert's design shows that you don't have to have decking, hammock, some pebbles and a fake seashore to make a garden feel coastal... it can be done more metaphorically and be equally convincing;
- remember that coastal plants have adapted to a harsh and salty environment, so some plants may not flourish in the sanctity of your domestic garden – consider using other plants that look and act like coastal plants but may be more tolerant of your favourable conditions;
- when considering what material to use in a garden, consider how it feels and how it looks against another material – so much of enjoying a garden is the visual and textural quality of the composition.

1 Evoking the mixed planting that can be found near the coast, both white and red valerian (*Centranthus ruber* var. 'Coccineus' and 'Albus') bring colour to this space, as do the spires of silver-leaved *Verbascum bombyciferum* 'Polarsommer'.

2 This secluded seating area looks over the rest of the garden. The back wall comprises horizontal painted timber slats supported by a steel frame while a planted 'green roof' offers protection.

DESIGNER Robert Myers

CONTRACTOR Willerby Landscapes

AWARD Silver-Gilt

CATEGORY Show Garden, 2011

SPONSOR Cancer Research UK

KEY WORDS straight lines; coastal; linear planting; different materials; seaside

IN A SENTENCE... A calming interpretation of a seaside design concept, using beautifully crafted materials.

3 To continue the coastal theme, 'bridges' were created from recycled timber taken from an Essex dock. Note how the rough texture contrasts with the smooth blocks of sandstone.

4 Coastal planting is in evidence throughout this garden – two primary examples are the vertical, spiky head of *Cordyline australis*, and the white-flowering form of tamarisk (*Tamarix gallica*). Both are good in seaside locations, and here provide shelter and vertical accents to the garden.

5 The curved bench makes a beautiful, material statement – sometimes it is worth spending extra money on a very special piece of furniture, that is both bench and sculpture. In this case, a single piece of oak has been carved by craftsman Jim Partridge, with a natural sanded finish.

6 One of the prettiest plants in this garden is that of a native maritime plant – sea thrift (*Armeria maritima*). By creating a row of it in a definite straight line, it reinforces the linear nature of this garden; its placement also mirrors that of it in nature, being near both rocks, pebbles and water (in this case, the water is housed within painted steel rills).

Every few years at Chelsea one of the show gardens features an iconic statement that is not only memorable for itself but also sums up the whole show. In 2007, garden designer Andy Sturgeon created just such a stir. His Cancer Research UK garden represented just how far sculpture and garden could combine: how the physical properties of a man-made oak structure, 30m (100ft) long, could seamlessly 'swim' through the air, as well as in and out of plants. It represented a symbiotic relationship of structure and flora seemingly living, moving and breathing together. Rarely has Chelsea seen such a combination work so successfully, while at the same time so strongly supporting the sponsor's message of 'together we will beat cancer'.

The designer is well known for creating modern, contemporary, highly styled gardens, mainly for well-off clients in the southeast of the UK and abroad. But he always manages to balance planting with hard materials. He adopts a similar approach for his show gardens, which are often jam-packed with plants, sublime construction and usually offset with some statement effect – maybe sculpture, a building or ingenious level changes. For many gardeners, his designs may seem unrealistic – in both budget and style – but look beyond the showmanship and you can see some really strong design working incredibly hard. There is much of this approach that can be transcribed to your back garden.

ELEMENTS THAT MIGHT BE USED IN A DOMESTIC SETTING:

- the combinations of plant shape, texture and colour, with each other and other built forms (sculpture, paving or building), creates interest, contrast and seasonal differentiation;
- by fully including such an incredible piece of sculpture from the outset, the planting and location of all the other elements within the space can be worked out;
- the delineation of areas by simple yew hedging brings a sense of formality and consistency across the space and also engenders a sense of visual respite from the rest of the planting;
- optimum use of space, which is vital for gardeners; here a linear path takes the visitor to a Japanese-inspired pavilion for contemplation and looking out across the garden. The garden seemingly moves, changes and swirls before your eyes, but if you take a closer look you can see that this space invites you to experience it. For most people, that is what a garden should do.

1 Hedging has been used at different levels (from waist height to shoulder height) to subdivide the space, while also acting as a simple green backdrop for the diverse range of plants at ground level.

2 This Portugese limestone path acts to 'calm' the space down and provides a feeling of light and respite from the textural and colour combinations elsewhere. With gardens that have many elements within them, such as this, it is often best to keep paths simple.

DESIGNER Andy Sturgeon

CONTRACTOR The Outdoor Room

AWARD Gold

CATEGORY Show Garden, 2007

SPONSOR Cancer Research

KEY WORDS oak sculpture; dense planting; texture; outdoor pavilion; contemporary; movement; flow

IN A SENTENCE... This sublime garden mixes colour, texture and shape to great effect, bringing hard and soft materials seamlessly together.

3 This oak sculpture, 30m (100ft) long, twists and entwines with itself and the planting below. Such a sculpture would cost a substantial part of a home garden budget (and would need more rigorous support), but its level of spectacle should inspire most creative gardeners. It was probably one of the most striking features of recent Chelseas.

4 An open-sided pavilion provides a place to relax – crucial for most gardeners. The black frames allow the structure to merge into the background, while the yellow chairs (created by Italian designer Paola Lenti with woven yachting rope) add a dash of vivid colour – here nicely offset by the dark yew hedges.

5 Different leaf form and colour – most notably, silver-leaved cardoons – have been used to maintain interest at ground level. Note, though, that in a real garden and after a summer's growth the plants will be nearer to head height so there will be quite a different feel to this space.

6 A beautiful *Cornus controversa* tree anchors the space, growing taller than the sculpture but with an airiness that allows light and sight into the garden. In successful gardens, the vertical plane is as balanced as the horizontal, as in this instance.

SUSTAINABILITY

Sustainability can be about so much more than processes, resources or applications. It can be creative, stimulating, challenging, funny, underhand or extreme.

There are some phrases that mark an epoch, that reflect a moment in time and that pinpoint public mood, fashion or cultural woes. The term 'sustainable development' is one such phrase. Coined in the early 1980s by the Brundtland Commission, which looked into concerns about the human environment and its natural resources, it is a phrase that has been debated by academics and the public alike.

The term 'sustainable development' means meeting the needs of the present generation without compromising those of future ones. Although this may sound simple enough, the reality at a local, national or global level is significantly more challenging. Nearly 30 years after the Brundtland Commission report, the need to live by such a tenet has never been more urgent.

So what relationship does sustainable development have with a six-day flower show such as Chelsea? On the face of it, not a lot. After all, critics cry, this is a show that swallows significant amounts of money and resources in order to make what is in effect a temporary exhibition. And they would be right if it were not for one thing – the people creating the show gardens and nursery displays. Nearly everyone involved with the show, from the Royal Horticultural Society to a first-time exhibitor, from colleges in the Lifelong Learning displays to gardening product manufacturers, is aware of their demands on the planet and is increasingly conscious about doing something about it.

Those exhibiting in any capacity at Chelsea know that no other gardening show has comparable notoriety or media attention. As a result, many of the show garden themes centre around sustainability issues: from water harvesting to recycled products; and from drought-resistant planting to photovoltaic lighting. Sometimes entire gardens focus on a sustainable issue (see case study, p170). At other times, it might be small elements in a show garden that suggest different ways of tackling things. Either way, the organisers require designers to explain how their gardens are sustainable.

Yet sustainability can be about so much more than processes, resources or applications. It can be creative, stimulating, challenging, funny, underhand or extreme. Designers and exhibitors revel in myriad possibilities, and rightly so. Sustainability needs to be imparted in a variety of ways and at different levels. For example, some gardeners may want to explore gardening organically, others may want to reduce their resource use (in terms of fertilisers or soil improvers). Some, who live in an urban environment have to plan and design their outside space minutely in order to get maximum sustainable use from it. Others, however, who may live in a larger rural garden, may not be so worried about space, but might find it easier to incorporate more composting facilities, fruit and vegetable growing, and diverse tree and plant selections. In other examples, some of the garden items (such as containers or paving) may be recycled or recyclable, while others may be considerably older but still in good condition. All these issues, and many more, meld into the pot of sustainability.

One of the many benefits of gardens is that together their sum is greater than the number of individuals. Also, studies such as the University of Sheffield's BUGS project (Biodiversity in Urban Gardens in Sheffield) have demonstrated the enormous repository

1 **Small things** can really help make a difference. Here paving slabs have been interspersed with loose stones, allowing rainwater to drip through to the ground below. This is a great way to assist in keeping ground water levels topped up.

2 **Water management** is a very real issue in an outside space, especially for garden designers and city planners. Reducing excess run-off and dealing with the ebb and flow of water levels can be 'built' into a design with prior consideration.

3 **Wildlife is crucial** to biodiversity, and in turn to enhancing a garden's sustainability. Here a bee collects pollen in a *Cirsium rivulare* 'Atropurpureum' flower.

3

that gardens can be for plants, wildlife and the environment in general. It is by designers reflecting on such findings, and then repackaging them for the benefit of the Chelsea audience, that such strong and important messages can be imparted.

For most gardeners, many of these issues are already everyday concerns. Therefore it is to the innovative ideas and new materials that gardeners should look when visiting Chelsea. Whether by planting green roofs (see p166) or using recycled car tyres as planters or raised beds; by introducing piles of logs to attract wildlife or including metal gabions filled with reclaimed industrial waste – designers will continue to explore the meaning of sustainability, and sustainable gardening. These are gardening realities that are set to be an increasingly important motif throughout many RHS Chelsea Flower Shows, and real life gardens, in the years to come.

EXPERT TIP
Nigel Dunnett Green roofs

‘ These are simply roofs that have had a layer of vegetation added to them. Garden sheds, porches, summerhouses, balconies, garages and small extensions all offer great potential for planting green roofs. Indeed, where garden or outdoor space is very restricted a green roof might be the only chance for bringing plants and wildlife into otherwise hard or built surroundings. The most important consideration for such a roof is how much weight the chosen building will support: it must comfortably take the weight of a person if it is to be strong enough to have a green roof planted on it; if you are in any doubt about this, do seek professional advice. The existing roof must also be waterproof. You can create a simple green roof by securing a pregrown mat of sedums over a pond liner on the roof surface, but it is preferable to plant individually into a generous layer of free-draining soil or potting compost on the roof. In addition to sedum species, many typical alpines such as *Dianthus* and thyme are excellent for green roofs, as are low-growing species tulips. Native wild flowers of chalk or limestone grassland, such as cowslip (*Primula veris*) and bird's foot trefoil (*Lotus corniculatus*), will increase the wildlife value of the roof. In partial shade, the range of plants can be increased to include alpine strawberries and ferns. Some watering may be necessary in very dry periods, and occasional weeding to remove unwanted plants. ’

Plant in a minimum soil depth of 7.5cm (3in) on the roof.

Green roofs can be positioned in full sun or partial shade.

Before planting, spread a pond liner over a suitably strong, waterproof roof to protect it from plant root damage.

1

Sustainability as part of the plan

With climate change and environmental awareness now part of everyday life for most people, how you use your garden will become an increasingly important question. It means that what you grow, how you grow it, where you get your materials from and how you maintain them are very real issues. Such an approach, however, does not require you to grow large areas of nettles and make way for hordes of rabbits. Many clients of garden designers are demanding that their outside space be as sustainable as possible, whether it be by the ethical sourcing of natural stone or by introducing water storage and irrigation. Whatever the demands are, many designers are in a great position to help clients realise their environmental dreams. By balancing human needs with environmental concerns, both designers and gardeners can help develop a symbiotic relationship from a shared piece of land.

OVERALL IDEALS WITH NEW IDEAS

From intelligent manufacturing techniques through to overall design, gardens can respond well to sustainable demands.

1 The planting combinations, use of space and balance of materials in this garden make it a great example of sustainability, even though it didn't set out to be so labelled. After Chelsea, it was to be relocated to a hospice for children – in itself, a great act of recycling and reuse.

2 This scheme balances the needs of people with that of a thriving plant and animal community. Contemporary detailing is softened by the lush planting, as well as by pools of water (hidden from view) and structures for nesting birds and insects (integrated into the walls).

3 Front gardens can make an invaluable contribution to a street environment, by introducing a mixture of planting and materials to strong effect, as in this scheme, which cleverly combines personal space with wider society benefit.

4 Concrete manufacturing is known as being environmentally 'unfriendly'. To overcome this, the designers here used an innovative technique to reduce the carbon footprint of concrete manufacturing while creating their contemporary design.

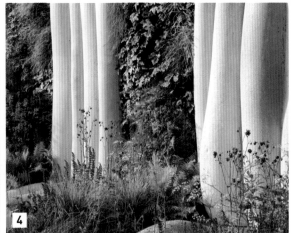

Attracting wildlife

Part of any successful ecosystem is the delicate balance of living organisms within a given area. For gardens to attract creatures – from the smallest insect to the largest garden mammal – they must provide food, shelter and the opportunity for that wildlife to make a home. You can easily help achieve this by introducing a range of habitats within your garden: from long grass to old pieces of decaying wood; from mixed planting to a pool of water. Turning your garden over to 'nature' while humans look on sounds for many people like ecospeak, yet that is far from the reality. What most gardeners, designers and Chelsea show gardens do is present a balance, where a range of materials are – by their very nature – different and are attractive to various parts of the wildlife spectrum. In so doing they are creating habitats that are well balanced, appealing to many creatures and continually sustainable as a result. Building and using a range of materials within a garden provides a host of opportunities for wildlife, whether by supporting different types of plants (and as a result food sources) or for nesting in inanimate objects such as walls and eaves.

LARGE AND SMALL, WILDLIFE FOR ALL

Whether planning a bee 'hotel' or an informal pond, wildlife encouragement should be an intrinsic part of any garden.

1 *Clematis*, rounded *Allium* heads and spires of white *Digitalis* are attractive, pollen-rich flowers for wildlife in late spring, and help give an informal, 'in tune with nature' feel to the space.

2 Keeping bees is an increasingly popular pastime, especially as bee populations across the world are in a state of decline. This garden shows how beautifully hives can be incorporated into a scheme.

3 These modern bird feeders have been set into a rendered wall – and should be squirrel-proof.

4 Another contemporary take, in the same garden as above, this time with solitary bee homes regularly spaced on a grey-blue wall.

5 A traditional bee-keeper's skep, made from twisted straw, sits on a milking stool.

6 Water is essential in any garden. This generous informal pond has shallow sides that allow wildlife easy access to the water, while the dense informal planting around it provides good cover for creatures.

Balancing aesthetics with nature's needs can be very challenging in a small garden. Good ideas include: native plants supporting a high level of biodiversity; pockets of water for visual impact and wildlife; and multistemmed trees for shade.

Nature Ascending, Angus Thompson & Jane Brockbank, 2009

Statements with sustainability

Most people interested in creating sustainable gardens focus on the actions required rather than the message itself. Yet what defines a 'sustainable garden'? Because there is no one answer, garden owners and designers have demonstrated in various ways their understanding of the term. For some, a sustainable garden could be the one in which they use only organic materials to make their plants grow; for others it may be that all materials are sourced from within the existing garden space; and for yet more people it may be about increasing biodiversity. Chelsea gardens respond to all of these interpretations, and propose ideas – large and small – from using bountiful local materials as paving through to planting swathes of wild flowers.

RIBBONS OF COLOUR

Sustainable gardens should be as visually exciting as any other garden; they needn't be dull drab places.

1 This clever urban backdrop screen, with a wildflower seed mixture sown in front, shows how easy it is to beautify city spaces. Bringing plants to the urban environment not only helps reduce the dominance of hard surfaces, but it also entices wildlife in and can help reduce the overall urban heat island effect.

2 Use of locally adapted plants alongside soil conservation, composting and a natural approach to pest control are key messages in this garden, and are easily adopted by gardeners. Such plants need less man-made fertilisers or soil improvers to make them grow, as they have evolved over time in harmony with local conditions.

DETAILED ELEMENTS

Small touches evoking a specific memory, or perhaps imparting a meaningful message, can be rewarding to undertake in a home garden and are quite often easy to achieve.

1 Two takes on sustainability: home-grown vegetables reduce 'food miles', while old keys contribute to the path's make-up as well as help to impart this garden's theme of improving services for people who are homeless.

2 Wildlife is not fussy about what it lives in, as this 'insect hotel' confirms. Succulent plants, egg boxes, old pipes, grasses, hollowed logs and even rolled up magazines – planted and non-planted – offer a sanctuary to the creatures we share our gardens with.

3 An old car windscreen protects these tomato plants from rain damage, while the glass helps warm the area below and so maximises cropping.

GREENING ROOFS FOR GREAT EFFECT

Green roofs can be made at home, maybe on a garden shed or garage. Always check the structural integrity of the building before planting.

1 This green roof – planted primarily with *Sedum* species – brings a nice visual treat to the garden and is a great improvement on a building's usual roof tiles or tarred felt.

2 With some detailed planning and an awareness of what materials are most appropriate, a green roof can be 'retrofitted' to most garden buildings.

3 No space should be considered too small for making a contribution to greening up the environment. Here a wheelie bin storage cupboard has green vegetation on its roof.

Green roofs and living walls

One of the most significant additions to some of the Chelsea show gardens in recent years has been green roofs and living walls. Both concepts originate from the same premise: that, instead of looking at hard materials such as roof tiles or concrete, why not grow plants on that surface. Other advantages are also recognised: green roofs help keep buildings cool in summer and warm in winter; they have great aesthetic appeal; wildlife benefits from more plants growing in a given space; and green roofs especially can help with water (rainfall) absorption and (on a large scale) reduce local air temperature in summer. Chelsea designers have really adopted living walls and green roofs, and it is disappointing that planners and architects have not done so more in the public realm. Questions remain about the long-term nature of these plantings, but that shouldn't put people off.

WALLS THAT 'BREATHE AND GROW'

Appropriate plant selection and maintenance needs are particularly important considerations when planting up a wall.

1 This interesting scheme adapted the concept of a green wall by planting shrubs on top of the retaining structure as well. The result is a piece of great design.

2 Purple-leaved *Heuchera* is of significant colour value in this living wall, which runs diagonally from the planting bed upwards.

3 Leaf form, texture and understanding appropriate growth habits are essential ingredients for a successful green wall, as can be seen here by the use of *Alchemilla mollis*, *Armeria*, *Heuchera* and sage.

Sustainable principles meet well-proportioned space in this garden. At its heart is a shipping container transformed into a studio; a green roof insulates it; pools hold rainwater; and stone walls offer different habitats for wildlife.

RBC New Wild Garden, Nigel Dunnett and The Landscape Agency, 2011

Whether your take on sustainability is social (getting people involved and employed for the long term) or environmental (selecting materials that are from a renewable resource), it is a term that increasingly has an effect on our lives. In this garden, sustainability is discussed in the form of communities, the places that allow people to live, to develop and to ultimately establish their type of home. This substantial show garden, covering 590 square metres was undertaken by garden designer Paul Stone and many other contributors, and gives a tangible example of how Government agencies, homelessness charities and prisons can work together for an improvement in people's lives.

IDEAS FROM THIS GARDEN FOR BEING SUSTAINABLE AT HOME:

- growing fruit and vegetables helps reduce the need to buy produce that may have been flown in from abroad, thereby reducing 'food miles';
- by working with different people (Government, the third sector and charities) you can help improve your community's growing space;
- recycling is all part of sustainability, so always consider reusing materials for alternative uses and let your imagination soar with the possibilities that previously used materials could be put to use for something else;
- sustainable gardening doesn't have to be dull or worthy – colour, aesthetics, taste and attention to detail are just as important as they are in any garden;
- consider the environmental benefits that gardens can offer, such as plants helping produce shade in summer which in turn reduces the heat in your house or garden;
- by growing a range of plant types in a garden (from crops to trees, shrubs to climbers) a range of wildlife can be welcomed which will help increase biodiversity;
- raised beds are an efficient way of growing crops, as they not only reduce the need to dig over existing soil, they allow fruit and veg to grow to their maximum potential in well-draining soil.

DESIGNER Paul Stone in partnership with Roderick James Architects, Jane Knight, Architecture sans Frontières-UK, BCHA (Bournemouth), Crisis Skylight (London), Look Ahead (London), Noah Enterprises (Luton), Providence Row (London), Supported Housing for Young People – (Ross-on-Wye), Stonham (Hull & Maidstone)

CONTRACTOR Teams from homelessness services and ex-offenders from across England and Wales

AWARD Silver

CATEGORY Show Garden, 2010

SPONSOR Homes and Communities Agency, Communities and Local Government, London Employer Accord

KEY WORDS communities; re-use; sustainability; recycling; growing produce; people; personalising space

IN A SENTENCE... A huge garden brimming with ideas, linking people to places, showing the value of horticulture at the heart of communities.

1 Wooden painted poles bring colour and structure to the garden, and add a sense of height which in turn makes the garden more visually interesting.

2 A great way of reusing large objects (such as these old wooden reels that would have held cables) is to give them a new lease of life – here they are acting as a potting table, as well as a place for displaying plants. Cleverly sited near the 'greenhouse' and raised beds, these 'tables' are a useful addition to any gardener's needs.

3 The 'greenhouse' is an ingenious way of reusing old plastic bottles (rather than letting them go into landfill or be recycled); they also give great insulation to the plants being grown inside. Even though this may not be a long-term alternative to a conventional greenhouse, it is a great idea for short-term crop protection.

4 Crops in pots broaden the range of things being grown – in this case herbs including purple sage.

5 Raised beds offer a great way of growing produce. The free-draining soil in such a bed aids speedy and successful growing, and the height of the bed can be raised to suit the gardener's needs – for example, taller beds can be created for those with physical disability so bending down can be minimised.

With more of the global population living in urban places, it is imperative that landscape architects, planners, architects, engineers and politicians grasp the urgent need to make cities as pleasurable to live in as possible. Infrastructure and planning are crucial, but so too are imaginative and practical solutions. By providing simple, useful and garden-friendly ideas here, Ark Design Management have shown that sustainability, environmental awareness and concern for urban developments can be visually stimulating... and environmentally beneficial.

Much of the current British work centred around greening urban environments – in terms of green roofs, public space seed mixtures and the use of sustainable resources – stems from work being undertaken in Sheffield, especially at the university of Sheffield. Research into understanding the urban environment, in tandem with the global scientific community's modelling information about climate change, is leading designers to understand better how gardens can help mitigate and adapt to fluctuations in weather. Just such a collaborative exercise was undertaken by the creators of this garden: horticulturist and ecologist Nigel Dunnett, architect Adrian Hallam and landscape architect Chris Arrowsmith. The result was an inspiring, enjoyable and successful garden.

CONSIDER THE IMPLICATIONS FOR DOMESTIC GARDENS:

- this garden aims to soak up, store and use every single drop of rainwater that falls onto the space – a key concern for anyone wanting to grow a range of plants in a limited outside space;
- planting and hard landscaping have been selected to deal with differing and sporadic levels of rainfall, so, for example, planting combinations are tough and some would need no irrigation in dry periods;
- wildlife, so vital to maintaining a healthy ecosystem, has plenty to feast upon, and endless opportunities in which to live (look at the central 'garden tower' to the left of the main picture);
- if buildings can be adapted to include a 'green' (planted) roof, then there are many possibilities. The benefit is not only visual – who would rather see roof tiles than a mixture of planting? – but also practical in terms of water storage, pollution absorption and planting diversity;
- the inclusion of water pools and rills – whether permanent or seasonal – creates visual interest and can also substantially boost wildlife.

This garden demonstrated many small-scale yet big-impact steps individuals can take to help counter the ongoing changes to our climate. Wouldn't it be a better place if all urban areas started to look a little like this?

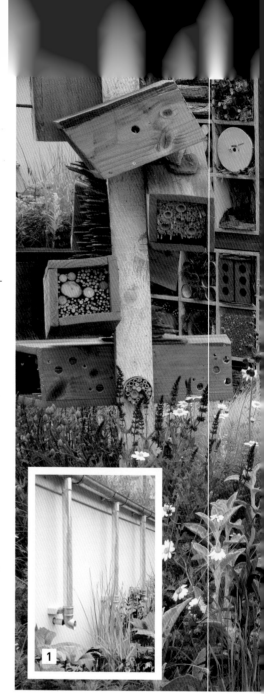

1 Drainpipes are used to direct any excess roof water onto the planting below. Green roofs help absorb and slow down the rate of storm water that would otherwise fall directly onto roads and buildings, and end up in the sewer system.

2 This 'living' tower provides plants and animals with space and a refuge. By incorporating a range of materials, sizes and textures, the attraction for fauna is maximised. In a home garden, a variety of unwanted materials could be used to dramatic effect.

DESIGNERS Ark Design Management
(Adrian Hallam, Chris Arrowsmith and
Nigel Dunnett)

CONTRACTOR Dendale, Galemain
Engineering, M&SE

AWARD Silver-Gilt Flora

CATEGORY Show Garden, 2009

SPONSOR Yorkshire Water, University of
Sheffield Alumni Fund, Green City Initiative
and Buro Happold

KEY WORDS sustainability; urban;
roof garden; eco-awareness; water
management; biodiversity

IN A SENTENCE... A great suite of water-
based ideas for planting and designing in
an urban environment.

3 A photograph of a city scene has been used as the backdrop to
this garden, to help give a sense of scale and reality to the design.
Considering the views beyond your garden, or the context in which your
creation sits, is essential, whether it be to maintain pleasant views or
to introduce plantings to block out eyesores.

4 A series of pools and rills occurs beyond this planting,
demonstrating how water can be incorporated into the smallest of
spaces, as well as the invaluable role plants have in water purification,
stormwater retention and for wildlife.

5 White-stemmed birches (*Betula utilis*) give height and a sense of
maturity at the back of the garden. These trees represent the diversity
of plants often seen in urban brownfield sites. At home, garden trees
are vital for interest and scale, but choose carefully as some are better
suited to smaller spaces than others.

6 The planting is a stylised meadow, with native and non-native plants,
several of which colonise urban wasteland, yet it has a beautiful and
'painterly' effect. In your garden, consideration of soil, aspect, wildlife
attraction and irrigation must be given to ensure that the maxim of
'right plant, right place' is adhered to at all times.

PRODUCTIVE GARDENS

Growing your own can be
one of the most satisfying
and rewarding parts of
any gardener's craft.

One of the most significant revivals that has taken place in recent years has been the renewed interest in 'growing your own' (GYO). As a reaction to the post-Second World War years of hardship and frugalness, and the excitement and technological innovation of the 1970s and 80s, home-grown fruit and vegetables had become something of a distant memory – until the past decade.

And what a revival it has been. Suddenly everybody is interested in growing some element of food, whether fruit, herbs or vegetables in a container, raised bed or in the ground. Allotment waiting lists run into years in some parts of the country, while schools and communities are being encouraged to come together to make space for food growing. Books, websites and magazines have focused on the topic for everyone from novice to the experienced. But where and how does the RHS Chelsea Flower Show fit into this – has it been able to keep up with this burgeoning interest? Indeed it has, by demonstrating very well the aesthetic and other benefits of including fruit and veg. The main challenge for nurserymen and designers when wanting to include crops in their gardens is the timing of the show. As a result many of the plants at Chelsea are forced.

By the third week of May, when the show takes place, fruit and vegetables are normally only in very early growth. Even with the most advanced growing conditions for making plants behave like it is actually July instead of May, it is still a considerable feat to be able to grow crops that are of a sufficient size, quality and number for show purposes. As ever with Chelsea show gardens, some years this growing trick can work brilliantly; in other years weather and bad luck may just be against the grower.

The end result is that productive gardening at Chelsea is demonstrated in many ways, and all of them usually applicable to a domestic situation. In some, the growing area occupies the whole garden, suggesting that a conventional space doesn't have to be confined to ornamental plants – it can be about seasonal vegetables, summer berries, culinary herbs or wildlife-haven fruit trees. At other times, designers include raised beds or containers that suggest smaller scale changes. But no matter the size or scale of the growing area, gardeners must always consider what they want to grow, how much they will want of it, and what soil type and aspect each crop will need. Once they have considered these essentials, the possibilities for including vegetables or fruit into the garden are endless.

One of the really exciting developments in productive growing over the past 30 years or so has been the expansion of seed and plant availability. Whereas in the middle of the 20th century people would have considered Brussels

1 Growing fruit, vegetables and herbs is a hugely rewarding undertaking, often with gardeners nurturing plants from a few packets of seeds to full-blown, harvestable crops.

2 Chelsea designers often incorporate fruit and vegetables to great effect in their show gardens, and in so doing recreate utopian images of how many of us might like our veg patch to be.

sprouts, cabbages and runner beans staple garden produce in the UK, gardeners are now treated to an international menu – from Thai or Asian vegetables to Mediterranean citrus; South American sweet potatoes to Italian salad leaves; bean sprouts to micro-, baby- or teen-leaf lettuce; and increasingly popular 'superfruits' (such as blueberries) to fruit trees grown on dwarfing rootstock, which are ideal for smaller gardens.

How they are used is also being explored. From mixing crops with ornamentals to growing serried ranks of unusual herbs, from planting strawberries in colanders to growing vegetables on vertical surfaces (see p182), designers' imaginations will continue to challenge perception and inspire supporters.

Increasingly, growing things – whether productive or ornamental – is being appreciated as an enjoyable pastime. Fruit or veg encourages children to get their hands dirty and give it a go. Ingenious and simple little touches come from the creative fingers of Chelsea designers, for children (see p184). Community-based projects, national media coverage and education-based guidance, such as the RHS Campaign for School Gardening, strive to reconnect children, and those from disadvantaged backgrounds, with the food they eat.

Ultimately, this is inspiration that Chelsea must provide. With continued interest in reducing 'food miles', the constant uncertainty on international food pricing and stability, and a greater awareness of the husbandry of food, gardeners will need shows like Chelsea to push boundaries and try new ideas. Coupled with the sheer beauty and interest in productive crops, this show will undoubtably demonstrate over the coming years that growing your own can be one of the most satisfying and rewarding parts of any gardener's craft.

3 Who says vegetables can't be ornamental? The bold lines of lettuce, chard and other summer greens create a dramatic statement, while having the added benefit of being productive.

Growing your own

The aesthetic appeal they can bring to a garden is often one of the forgotten benefits of growing fruit and veg. All that energy, colour, shape and texture with different growth habits, can be found in one small area, bringing together produce that originated from different parts of the world into your back garden. The other self-evident benefit is that with a bit of foresight, due care and attention and some luck, most gardeners can establish and raise crops successfully to produce home-grown fare. Taste, freshness, quality, reduced 'food miles' and a huge amount of satisfaction combine to make growing your own a great way to spend some or all of your gardening time.

1

EXPERT TIP
Jekka McVicar
How to grow herbs

❛ As a general rule, Mediterranean herbs such as thyme (*Thymus vulgaris*), sage (*Salvia officinalis*), oregano (*Origanum vulgare*), savory (*Satureja montana*) and French tarragon (*Artemisia dracunculus* French) like to be planted in full sun in a well-drained soil. The reason full sun is required is that it is the sun that brings the herbs' essential oils to the surface of the leaf, and it is these oils that make the herbs taste so good in the kitchen. An important tip for keeping these herbs productive for regular use in the kitchen is to cut the plants back after flowering. This will encourage new growth and, with the exception of the tarragon as it is herbaceous, will give you leaves for use in the winter months. Increasingly, gardeners are intermingling herbs with their ornamental plantings, and there are many different selections of herbs to link them in visually. ❜

This 'herb wheel' is a great addition to any garden, bringing together thyme, salvia, oregano and parsley for use in the kitchen.

STYLE TO SUIT ALL TASTES

Productive gardens, large or small, can balance both visual style and personal growing preference.

1 Blue-painted planters of different heights visually co-ordinate a range of crops, from leeks to courgettes, beetroot to apple trees.

2 This formal, classic scheme unusually uses low, woven-willow-edged raised beds in conjunction with high-quality paving, and a beautiful greenhouse (for establishing young plants) in the distance.

3 A herb bed on top of an outside storage cupboard is a simple idea that is not only useful but also clean and contemporary in style.

Raised beds

Originally introduced into areas of poor or heavy soil, raised beds were built above ground level and filled with new, better soil, so as to allow crops to grow well. However, over time this practical response to poor soil has almost become the norm, with more and more gardeners opting for raised beds to contain their productive gardening. Not only is soil quality much easier to manage in a raised bed, but maintenance issues of keeping edges neat and weeding are also convenient because the beds are higher off the ground. In true Chelsea fashion, designers continue to push the creative boundaries of what materials constitute a raised bed, and what can be grown within them.

FROM THE GROUND UPWARDS

Consider the amount of growing space you need for your crops, and then devise raised beds to meet that requirement.

1 These herbs (rosemary, thyme, sage and lemon balm) are well set off by a curved blue metal planter.

2 Chives and bronze fennel, in the nearest woven-willow-edged raised bed, with cardoons in the second bed, combine for a visual feast.

3 A raised, plinth-like planter doubles up as a bench and somewhere to fill with productive vegetation – in this instance a 30-year-old, late-flowering apple tree growing from within it.

4 A contemporary take on veg growing in a small space – a steel tray, filled with mature lettuce.

5 Strong colour and foliage textures abound in this small space held together by a white painted wall.

Gardening for a beautiful bounty

The joy of growing your own can bring different ages, cultures and abilities together. Just as with ornamental planting, productive gardening can represent your personal interests; it can reflect the style of your overall garden, respond to needs and tastes, and can help you understand the relationship between garden and soil. In all, productive gardening can be a hugely rewarding experience, where successes are greeted with glee and delight, and failures met with a steely determination to try something different next time. Growing your own is not always easy, and problems are often encountered, but when a seed germinates or your first tomato is ready to pick, it brings a smile to even the most experienced of growers.

GETTING THE MOST FROM YOUR SPACE

Maximising use of space is crucial if a small garden is to yield a crop of fresh and healthy plants.

1 This novel kitchen garden concept explores the possibility of growing fruit and veg in a small space, on walls and surfaces, really hitting home the link between 'kitchen' and 'garden'.

2 Many vegetables, here including lettuce, can be grown closely together for immediate and ongoing harvesting.

3 With well-used space and a lot of hard work, a produce-laden garden can be achieved, ensuring garden owners have a fresh supply of food for many months of the year.

4 Lettuce, beans and tomatoes jostle together in a small corner of this garden and are enhanced by a sunny sunflower.

Contained excitement

Increasingly, those gardeners with small outside spaces are being offered the opportunity to share in the 'grow-your-own revolution'. Whether it be by choosing specially bred cultivars that grow smaller, or via growing systems that use soil and water to maximum effect, the owner of a small garden can really get stuck into growing produce. And the beauty of veg, especially, is that it doesn't care what it is being grown in – a row of lettuces in an old plastic container will be just as happy as they would be in the ground, as long as feeding, watering and husbandry are kept to the normal standard. Growing produce in containers is also a great way of involving children, allowing them to garden at their physical height, as well as in defined areas that are not too onerous. Whatever your passion, or your palette, growing your own in a container is a viable, enjoyable way of running a kitchen garden.

CONTAINERS CAN BRING A WEALTH OF GROWING OPPORTUNITY

No matter what the container is and where it is placed – on a windowsill or in a courtyard – it can be used to grow fresh produce in any garden.

1 Hard pruned fig trees in terracotta pots lend height and structure, and are also a great textural addition with their glossy green leaves.

2 Cress in old egg shells is just one novel idea to get children involved with growing and is a great way of introducing them to gardening.

3 When growing vegetables and fruit in containers people normally think of raised beds or terracotta pots. Sleek contemporary containers give a different look but they still have the same productive outcome.

4 Pot-grown citrus plants can be brought outdoors during the summer months to help fruit ripen, as they do best in a sunny warm position.

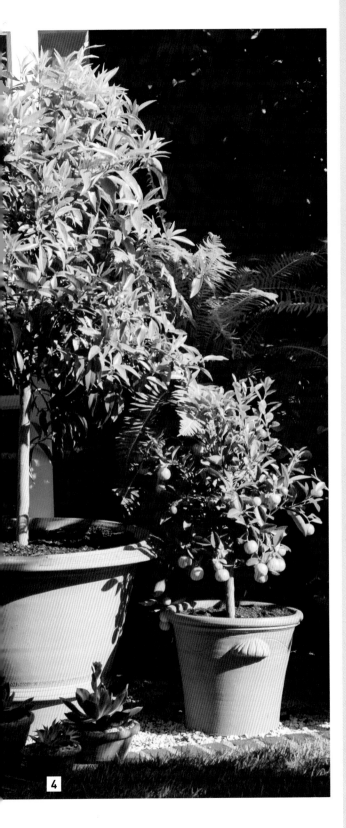

4

EXPERT TIP
Jekka McVicar
Planting up a container
for summer salad crops

❛ Salad rocket (*Eruca vesicaria* subsp. *sativa*), dill (*Anethum graveolens*) and mustard (*Brassica juncea*) are all great salad herbs that can be easily raised from seed and grown in a container. The trick is to choose a planter large enough to grow a crop for cutting; an ideal size is 23cm (9in) wide by 18cm (7in) high, or 5 litres/1 gallon, or larger. Fill with compost and water well, then sow the seeds and cover lightly with more compost. Set the container in a sheltered warm spot that is shaded from the midday sun. Once you start cutting your salad, feed the plants every week with a balanced liquid fertiliser. This will help them to develop productive succulent growth. ❜

Growing vegetables in raised planters gives physically easy access while allowing soil to be free-draining and easily improved.

Getting a message across is often a key requirement for a sponsor, but it can sometimes get 'lost in translation' in the actual garden. Not so here. This immaculately executed display reflected the sponsor's vision for high-quality materials, organic principles and clean design. For some, this was not a garden but an idealised version of an agrarian landscape comfortably existing side by side with a potager and outdoor kitchen. But, at Chelsea, such an approach can make a garden, and this fine example showed how big design statements – a 'field' of green wheat, raised vegetable beds and a green-roofed building – not only give inspiration but also reflect a deeper ethos.

This was the first time that the design partnership of del Buono Gazerwitz had entered Chelsea. Their design style of clean lines and simple spatial combinations translated well into this space. The balance of areas, combinations of materials and strong ethos underlying the show garden's creation reinforced a message that any gardener at home can undertake. At the core, though, was the need to be consistent and dogged; the designers and sponsor here wanted to remind gardeners of the 'vital importance of nurturing the soil and preserving it for future generations', and they have made sure every detail rings true to that.

MUCH CAN BE LEARNED FROM THIS SCHEME:

- even in a relatively small space (210 square metres/250 square yards), you can have two distinct areas: the wheat 'field' (see inset) and a vegetable garden;
- by including two quite different spaces, the plot can feel a lot bigger than its crude dimensions suggest;
- the use of quality materials – such as the raised vegetable beds or green roof on the outdoor building – reinforce a message of longevity and craftsmanship;
- a 'rural' style can easily be created in a contemporary and modern way;
- having, in close proximity, a cooking area, fresh produce and a building happily facilitates 'outdoor living';
- green roofs can be applied to many buildings, providing visual interest as well as environmental benefits;
- fruit and vegetables can take a lot of work (especially to look this good) so be prepared for some failures, some successes and a lot of hard work.

1 Rustic-style, woven plant supports materially link with the raised beds, allowing tomatoes to grow up through them. Such vertical accents are needed to give scale and drama to this beautiful sea of vegetable and fruit growing. As most vegetables are grown in just one year, the following year something completely different could grow up the supports: maybe some runner beans, climbing gourds or ornamental sweet peas.

DESIGNER Tommaso del Buono and Paul Gazerwitz; Spencer Fung Architects

CONTRACTOR Brambles Garden Landscapes

AWARD Silver-Gilt Flora

CATEGORY Show Garden, 2008

SPONSOR Daylesford Organic

KEY WORDS country; rural; quality details; contemporary feel; outdoor kitchen; craft

IN A SENTENCE... A two-part garden, linking the wider landscape with productive horticulture, underpinned by quality construction.

2 The healthy, diverse and interesting range of crops – from chives to cardoons, parsley to cabbages – contributes to the success of this space, as does the simple but beautifully executed design. Many people would deem this their idealised vision of a vegetable garden.

3 This outdoor fireplace could be used for cooking freshly harvested produce or more ornamentally as an outdoor fire, ready to be relaxed next to after eating a plentiful meal. Either way, it adds a grand focal point to the wall and the whole growing area, and it reinforces the link between organic crop growing and culinary uses.

4 A rough, hoggin-like path divides the raised growing beds, bringing a sense of gridded formality to all the energy being displayed by the crops. Paths and access are crucial for veg plots: make sure the paths between beds are big enough to allow for a smooth passage. In many instances this may need to be wide enough for a wheelbarrow.

5 A simple grass path in the front end of the garden leads up to a hand-made gate (decorated with a rustic heart shape) and on into the productive garden. Although still underpinned by organic principles, in the front garden the designers show us the agrarian landscape, a field of green wheat gently swaying in the wind.

LIGHTING

Chelsea gardens show that whole new effects can be created outside by well-planned, and responsibly used, light.

The concept of the 'room outside' has been around since the 1960s, when leading garden designer John Brookes established it as a term that gardeners could understand. In a sense, the term 'room outside' gave people permission to consider their gardens as spaces that could be embellished, beautified or used for relaxation. As a result they became places for creative expression.

Nowhere is this decorative trend more true than with the development of garden lighting. By its very nature, using lights in a garden extends the amount of time that can be spent outdoors – it allows owners to use their outside space at the flick of a switch. Sitting in your garden, surrounded by some well-positioned lights, enjoying the evening ambience, can create a whole new relationship with your environment. At night – or early in the morning – the mass and voids, structure and form, colour and texture can become 'invisible' because they are not illuminated; and the end result is something quite different.

So what sort of lighting should be considered for a garden, and how have Chelsea designers included it? In recent years innovation has allowed them to really experiment with lighting; long gone are the days of large coloured bulbs pointing directly at a tree. As well as mains-fed lights, photovoltaic lighting (powered by the sun) has improved greatly in recent years, and substantially in design – originally their light was a musky yellow, but now a much clearer white light is given out.

Nowadays, gardens can have 'washes' of light to highlight the important, add drama to the ordinary and illuminate the necessary. Chelsea show gardens use just such principles to great effect (see case study, p200) – on a dramatic sculpture here or a water feature there. And in a way, it is this understanding of how lighting can enhance and improve a space that has 'powered' the substantial technical advancement in garden lighting. Chelsea gardens show us, as does the lighting industry, that whole new effects can be created outside by intelligent use of light.

A number of considerations are crucial before lighting your garden: you must think about which areas you want or require illuminated, and how that might be achieved; garden illumination isn't about having as many lights outside as possible. In addition, consideration should be given to neighbours or adjacent spaces. So too should there be concern for wildlife and energy use, especially if the lights are to be kept on at night. You should mix into the blend the need to plan and design for trunking and wiring, as well as the necessity that garden lighting must be fitted by a qualified professional electrician.

But what gardeners gain from Chelsea is, as is so often the case, a bag full of ideas. Over the years, the inclusion of lighting in show gardens has increased, to the point now where it is possible that most displays will include some lights. Undertaken well, and with attention to detail, lighting gardens can be an art form in itself. A little time working out what you want to illuminate, and by how much, will substantially increase your enjoyment when you sit down – one night – in your garden surrounded by washes of beautiful light.

1 **Accentuating the vertical** form in a garden is a common use of garden lighting. Here, a light placed at the base of a silver birch not only illuminates the branches and structure of the tree but also highlights the clean white trunk.

2 Coloured lighting can be used to strong effect in gardens, though consider its use carefully – the 'wrong' type or application of a colour can look tacky. Here the folds in the sculpture help reduce the block of colour, adding texture and shadows to the overall impression.

3 The lighting techniques in this classical view can be applied to a range of garden settings: the urn in the foreground uplit, with the same technique mirrored on the sculpture behind. They focus attention on exactly what you – the creator – wants visitors to see.

ALL PART OF THE PLAN

Whether lighting a building or a tree, consider how and what role you need garden lights to play.

1 This clever scheme continues the atmospheric lighting from the outside space to the indoor garden room.

2 An ambient feel to this seating area has been created by backlighting the planting behind while focusing other lights onto the 'sails' above.

3 With a detailed approach to illumination, such as here, you can single out important parts of the night-time garden.

Illuminating effects

Lights can be used in two principal ways in a garden: as a means of illuminating a specific object (see p194) or as a facility for shedding light across a larger area. For the latter, it is necessary to work out exactly what you want to be illuminated, how that effect may take place and what any by-products of that lighting may be. For the former, identify how you want the object lit and consider how that element may change appearance when artificially illuminated.

It is now well understood that when a large single light is placed in a garden its illumination is both unsympathetic and visually unappealing within the area. Therefore, it is far better to understand how light works and what mood and ambience you want your garden to have at night-time. If possible, use freestanding lights while determining your scheme; then when you are ready to install them permanently, you can be sure that your desires will come true.

EXPERT TIP
Tony Craddock Light sources

❛ The four main types of primary light sources commonly used for gardens are as follows:

- LED (light emitting diode) offers a wide choice of colours: white, blue, red, green, amber and colour-change versions. The bulbs have a long life, are cool to touch and have low running costs.
- High-pressure sodium is complementary to reds and yellows (such as red-leaf copper beech and *Prunus* trees). Sandstone and traditional brickwork also benefit from sodium lighting.
- Halogen creates a warm atmosphere and is associated with the natural environment. Despite its shorter life, it is the best choice for illuminating domestic plants and foliage.
- Metal halide is probably the best 'all rounder' light source, with its relatively long bulb life as well as its light spectrum resembling natural daylight, which makes it an especially good choice for revealing objects in their true colours. ❜

[above] LED lights illuminate a flight of steps, providing gentle guidance rather than blinding people as they pass through the space.

[left] This halogen spotlight uplighter is a discreet but effective way of focusing onto a tree or sculpture.

3

Lighting the specific

The main challenge when lighting a garden is understanding exactly what will and will not be illuminated. In the daytime this is difficult to predict, so trial and error are necessary when finalising your lighting scheme. To get the best from your garden, a range of styles and applications can be used, from specific small-scale spotlighting to washes of colour against a wall or flight of steps. Many lighting appliances can be bought from local shops or the internet, but make sure that they are fitted by trained electricians who understand the appliances.

DEFINITION IN WORK

Colour can be achieved in different ways, either by the bulb light itself or by the illumination of a coloured object.

1 Simple, ground-level highlights, here in blue-mauve, make the natural white of the birch bark have an almost ghostly appearance.

2 This unusual and substantial sculpture is enhanced by night-time illumination; note how the colours change as it falls on different parts of the creation, using shadows and intensity to great effect.

INTO SHARP RELIEF

Whether it is a spotlight on a tree or a path light illuminating steps, a range of products can be used to enhance the garden.

1 As night falls, artificial lights begin to illuminate a vegetable planter and associated wall. Their low level, on the ground plan and within the planting, gives a soft and relaxed atmosphere, and makes the whole space feel particularly accessible during evening.

2 This Japanese-inspired lantern provides a diffused light in a dark corner. Note how much more subtle the lighting effect is here, when compared with more self-conscious spotlights. Always try to hide or at least reduce from view an appliance's bulb – its glare can ruin a night-time illumination.

3 Glass tiles lit from underneath the floor of a patio reveal their interesting and considered detail. The gentle light created helps people move over the space easily.

EXPERT TIP

Tony Craddock
Employing an electrician

Consulting a qualified electrician is the best way to ensure that you get exactly the garden lighting scheme you want.

❛ Garden lighting can be complicated and should be done by qualified professionals. Indeed, in many countries it is now illegal for anyone other than a qualified electrician to install and maintain a lighting scheme (in the UK, this is known as 'Part P' of Building Regulations). Such electricians can be sourced through professional trade associations. Be clear with them about what you want, and always check on how long the job is likely to take. Before giving the go-ahead for the lighting scheme, you should consider the implications that armoured trunking will need to be laid deeply enough so as not to be caught when digging over a bed. For a short time, this may mean moving plants. You will also need easy access to circuits and primary switches located indoors. ❜

Aqua dramatics

In everyday life, water and electricity do not normally mix. But thanks to great advancements in technological engineering – plus some clever visual trickery – water can be illuminated to create amazing garden scenes. The effect can be startling, bold, refined or enchanting. The most common appliances are submerged lights, placed below the water level, whereby depth and a bright white light can be introduced. Other lighting techniques involve the careful placement of appliances under or within fountains or jets; in more pared-down schemes, lights can be used to give a discreet wash of colour near or on the water's surface. Fitting such lighting requires a competent professional electrician who understands the demands of the lighting, and water feature, throughout the gardening year. Ensure maintenance is easy to carry out on fuse boxes, switches and appliances.

1

2

[right] Uplighters can be set within a lawn so that they shine directly up and underneath a tree canopy – the effect is eye-catching, contemporary and pleasantly welcoming.

[far right] Night-time lighting can be used to highlight details (here, a tree trunk) that during the daylight hours might be overlooked.

EXPERT TIP
Tony Craddock
Lighting techniques

❝ A wide range of light fixtures and styles can give an array of night-time views. Consider what you want the effect to be, and how the light sources may practically be subsumed into the garden. Lighting can be used to make different impacts:

- Downlighting replicates the way light (sunlight) is perceived, and it is especially effective when used in structures such as pergolas or from canopies.

LIGHTING THAT EBBS AND FLOWS

Whatever the effect required, garden lighting is one way in which you can make a water feature come alive.

1 The drama of the arched water feature is augmented by the illumination of the circular pool below, while the back lighting against the canopy in the corner encourages night-time use.

2 The true magic of this unusual glass seat comes at night, when the LED lights are turned on to give it a watery glow. The light contrasts with the grasses in front and the tree behind.

3 Diamond-sawn paving slabs appear to float above the water, their form and texture accentuated by the subtlety of light – the sources of which are hidden in this view.

4 Full-on shock and awe are created in this two-tier water feature. The top pool and jets seem to be burning bright white, while the vertical waterfall glows blue. The net result is a great water feature that can be appreciated throughout the whole evening.

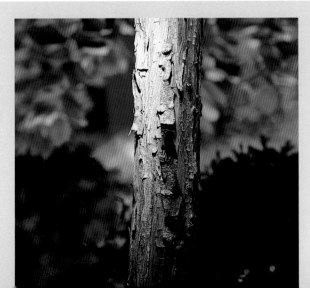

- Uplighting – when a lighting fixture is placed under an object such as a tree or sculpture – creates an overall wash of illuminated space. Recessed uplight fixtures are very discreet.
- Spotlighting is a direct lighting technique used to illuminate important features such as statuary.
- Path lighting is generally subtle and is for illuminating the horizontal plane; it gives direction and helps people avoid tripping on potential hazards such as steps.
- Silhouetting, as seen in nature at sunset, is when an object is between the viewer and setting sun; use wide-beam light sources placed behind planting or objects to create this effect. 〞

The role of lighting in bringing this garden into night-time use has been executed with style and drama. Cold blue accentuates the planting at ground level and lights the sculptural daisies, while clear 'white' lights make the garden building fully usable.

The Oceânico Garden, Diarmuid Gavin and Sir Terence Conran, 2008

Lighting is an addition to a garden that many people desire. But to be truly successful, the products that create the effect need to be discrete and cast light in such a way that there is no glare or visual intrusion to the way you enjoy an outdoor space. None of us would want to sit outdoors with an intruder light bearing down on us – it spoils the atmosphere, and makes being part of a night-time garden unspecial. This garden however shows that with a bit of consideration and care, where a light is placed – and what effect it will achieve once on – can have stunning results.

Designer Robert Myers has created a space surrounded by a louvered timber cloister which throws light and shadows both at night and in the day. The dominant double-height roof gives an airy, almost cathedral-like quality to the space, which makes the garden feel much bigger than it actually is. By defining some areas with lights, and leaving other parts in shadow, Robert has 'stage managed' the effect of the lights creating a night-time ambience of their own.

WHEN CHOOSING GARDEN LIGHTING:

- consider the effect you want to achieve – is the lighting to create a relaxing atmosphere or is it more practical, for defining a path or working area?
- when the lights are turned on at night, anticipate how they will marry with the textures and colours they are illuminating – here, Robert has up-lit panels of limed ash which cast shadows and shapes of their own;
- be clear about what really needs to be lit – too much and the space can feel like being under search lights but too little and the dominance on the dark spaces will overpower the lit feature;
- work with any good lighting retailers or suppliers who should allow you to install some of the lights temporarily, so that you can think about your needs – move lights around, consider different strengths of light, look at the practicality of their housing and where the cabling can be run from;
- consideration of neighbours and wildlife is paramount, so only use the lights for the time you are actually in the garden (rather than leaving them on all night) and illuminate only the areas that need illuminating.

1 The whiteness of the peony (*Paeonia* 'Jan van Leeuwen') adds an interplay of light and dark in this garden; so too the dark mounds of box in containers on the far right of the space. The texture of the planting, and its colour, are all part of the designer's consideration for how this space looks when lit.

2 The seating area is paved with beige Chinese granite, sawn and finely textured. Note how one of the roof lights throws a clearly-defined edge of light onto the smooth paving.

DESIGNER Robert Myers

CONTRACTOR Willerby Landscapes

AWARD Gold

CATEGORY Show Garden, 2010

SPONSOR Cancer Research UK

KEY WORDS uplighters; woodland planting; outdoor space; vertical timber slats; circular water; Chinese granite paving; calm.

IN A SENTENCE... A contemporary outdoor space that is as beautiful in the day as it is at night, enhanced by clever and specific lighting.

3 The timber pergola instantly lends height and depth, while small, discrete uplighters illuminate a few of its tulipwood louvers (painted black, and then fixed onto a steel frame). The black paint, backlit by the lights creates the clever visual illusion of space.

4 At the centre piece of this seating area is a series of wall-hung panels of limed ash; the differing sizes create an abstract relief. By using ground-level uplighters underneath it, a sculptural interplay of light and shadow has been achieved.

5 Even though this garden seems to use a multitude of straight lines (from the timber pergola to the cut of the paving), at its centre is a simple circular water feature that brings an organic shape to the space. The small white waterlily (*Nymphaea* 'Pygmaea Alba') helps to soften the water feature.

6 Chelsea gardens often have beautiful furniture to help finish off the space – here, individual armchairs made by B&B Italia. Furniture style and colouring are considered as well as planting and hard materials.

ART IN THE GARDEN

In essence, this is an artistic display or creation that uses materials to symbolise, highlight or adorn your garden.

For thousands of years, mankind has personalised and adorned his immediate surroundings. From long-standing symbolic religious embellishments to seasonal displays, people have used both the precious and the commonplace to give identity to a space. Whether it be for a day or for a lifetime, gardeners and artists alike have used a vast array of materials for serious and humorous purposes.

In a modern context, such a basic human desire to decorate, augment or personalise a garden has never been more apparent. From mass-market, garden-centre products to bespoke pieces of one-off artwork, consumers are increasingly buying artefacts that can be sited outside. The RHS Chelsea Flower Show demonstrates this only too well; there, the gardens generally include artwork to support or define a design, and there are also many sundry stands displaying sculpture, water features or furniture.

So, what can be considered 'art in the garden'? In essence, it is an artistic display or creation that uses materials to symbolise, highlight or adorn your garden. As with paintings, artistic appreciation is highly personal, so for some people a collection of old-fashioned terracotta pots lined up on a windowsill would define 'art'; for others, it may be the inclusion of expensive, one-off sculptures displayed to maximum effect. In another garden, stone figures that you chance upon may be more subtle than a row of flags fluttering boldly in the wind, yet the enjoyment and appreciation they give may be the same – but for different people. It is this breadth of consumers that Chelsea manages to relate to.

It is unsurprising that many sections of society are wanting to purchase and enjoy such a range of art, especially now that they are becoming more media savvy, with the ever-swirling mass of information the internet provides. Television and papers too are exploring design in much greater detail.

Show gardens tend to include artworks either as adornment and addition, or as an integral part of the overall design. For the former, it is perhaps easier to see how lessons can be learned for the gardener. In such gardens, designers may include a water feature that ebbs and flows on a constant rhythm; a sculpture that relates to surrounding flower colour or hard landscaping; or a piece of wall-mounted *trompe-l'oeil* that acts as a focal point. These are one-off elements, bought, placed and viewed primarily as single pieces.

More challenging, both spatially and financially, is the inclusion of artworks to help define an entire space. Consideration must be given as to what you want the artwork to achieve in the space; what it might look like; how you will relate to it over time (and how it will weather); as well as practical concerns such as security and fixings.

The role producers and manufacturers play in inspiring the gardening public should not be underestimated. Not only do they display what can be bought, but in so doing they suggest ideas that people might otherwise have not been aware of. Mirrors, for example, can be placed in a garden to extend the feeling of space, as long as they are located in a suitable place and reflect features worthy of highlighting; sculptures, likewise, can be placed anywhere in a garden, giving a bold- or low-key statement. Paint effects (either as wall colour or subtle highlights) can bring a new dimension to a space, as can recycling materials to create visual interest.

1

1 Using large pieces of artwork in a garden can take courage, but when dealing with organic, beautiful shapes, it is often easy to find (or create) a suitable location. These stone sculptures, by Peter Randall-Page, harmonize well with the simple tree trunk of *Parrotia persica*, the clean lines of the hedge behind and the gravel below.

2 Discreet pieces of art are becoming increasingly common in gardens, but how they are positioned, and how they are lit, are important concerns. Here the bowing man looks as if he is ready to smell the white-flowered lily next to him.

A sense of 'stage set' is also evident at the RHS Chelsea Flower Show – the odd unplanted terracotta urn here, or a collection of twigs there – to give an impromptu but artful contribution. The net result is an air of creativity at Chelsea that stimulates the senses and gets gardeners thinking about their next purchase or their own home-made artwork.

In financial terms, garden artworks can range from those that are totally free to those costing thousands of pounds. There are now myriad artisans, creators and designers willing to work with clients to produce whatever is required, whether it be made from wood, steel, bronze, glass, Perspex or other materials. However, art in the garden should be about more than flash statements or 'cheque-book gardening': it should reflect the spirit of the owners, relate to their likes and dislikes, and be just as important as hanging a picture above a fireplace indoors. What matters is that you enjoy the artwork for what it is. Whether a painted wall or bronze, life-size horse's head, a highly decorated dividing screen or a slowly weathered stone sculpture... artworks in the garden should be as individual as the individuals owning them. And for those people, Chelsea never disappoints.

3 When combined, materials – here, metal and water – can substantially increase the sum of a sculpture's parts. This filigree leaf seems to float gently on the smooth water surface, belying the actual complexities of ensuring that this balancing act is executed to perfection.

4 Large sculptures such as this are dominant focal points in a garden, and need to be sited with care and attention. Note how the screen behind softens the overall effect, blurring the depth and edges of the glass mass, thereby reducing its overall impact.

Location, location

How and where you position a particular sculpture are probably as important considerations as the actual style of the artwork itself. Sometimes gardeners have a specific area that would welcome the adornment of an artwork, but it can take a long time to find the appropriate piece. At other times, just as with a plant in a garden centre or a painting in a gallery or an art exhibition, the sculpture is an impulse buy, as you seize the moment and acquire the piece just because you love it. Either way, there are endless styles, sizes, materials and functions that will suit a range of gardens. To fully maximise the relationship between artwork and location, consider the style of your garden, the architecture of surrounding buildings and what the atmosphere of your private space is – these concerns may help you focus on the type of sculpture that is appropriate for your particular garden.

1

2

SCULPTURES IN FINE FOCUS

By including sculptures (large or small, temporary or permanent) in a garden you can add a welcome visual stimulus to an area.

1 An amazing mammoth sculpture, though not actually life-size, seems to be lurching forwards as it emerges from the trees behind. In doing so, it demonstrates not only the sublime composition of the artwork, but also how the backdrop of trees helps set the scene for dramatic effect.

2 This model of a Mini convertible on top of a wooden die is at the other end of the artwork scale. It makes playful reference to the garden's narrative, which is linked to a well-known family board game.

3 The magnificent horse's head has been plated together by the artist, giving it an industrial metallic feel. A thing of beauty for many, it is a bold display of artistic endeavour.

4 Taking cues from the way an art gallery would display its subjects inside a building, these three plinths are home to different sculptural artworks. Note how the white backing panels help show off the works to greater effect.

5 Although appearing much more understated, this metal keyhole design in fact has three roles: it acts as a piece of art in itself; it creates an entrance for the visitor to pass through into the garden; and it frames a view to the sculptural moon at the far end of the space.

6 Not everything at Chelsea is big and expensive: these simple coloured glass sculptures can brighten any window ledge, container or outdoor planting. En masse the colours, and the light they create, are particularly effective.

Sculpture for strong effect

So much of using a sculpture successfully depends on how the overall garden design is put together, and how the visitor is encouraged (or directed) to view the scene. Sometimes sculptures can make bold visual statements, overtly showing that they exist; at other times they are much more subtle, partly hidden in foliage or maybe changing in texture or colour over time. It may sound unnerving, but putting a piece of artwork into the wrong location can be devastating – not only to the garden but also to the piece in question. For new gardens, it may be easier to start off with an artwork and then plant or decorate around it; for more mature gardens a chance gap in a hedge or among plants may warrant the creative addition. Either way, practical considerations such as how the piece is to be fixed to a secure base (especially in times of heavy rain, strong winds or against theft) are also important.

PURPOSE AND STYLE

Given appropriate forethought as to where the artwork is to be sited, the gardener's artistic intention can be well satisfied.

1 A brushed steel sculpture is beautifully enhanced by the surrounding metal pergola and numerous plants growing around it.

2 This fun take on society in the 1980s is both a visual sculpture and a water feature. The planting softens the effect (but less so in winter).

3 Time for tea? Sometimes the intention of sculptures can be to raise a smile or reaction in the garden visitor, which is no bad thing.

4 David Harber's sculpture is surrounded by lush green planting. The stainless steel elliptical disc reflects and refracts light, adding a completely different visual experience in this part of the garden.

EXPERT TIP

Philip Nash
How to position a sculpture

❝ When considering where to site sculpture in a garden, decide whether you wish to create a focal point where your eye is drawn to pause on the piece before leading to the vista beyond, or if the focal point is to be the final destination. Is your sculpture to blend in with its surroundings or is it to stand out? And in that position will it match the surrounding style, be it classic, contemporary, natural or romantic? Look for a 'natural' place to set an artwork – one that feels right and best creates the effect you are seeking. For example, you may want the sculpture to be in a prominent position that will command attention, or you may prefer your garden visitors to discover an artwork placed off to the side (within a planted border). An artwork set in front of a wall or hedge will give it presence and/or provide a solid backdrop; if you don't have a suitable backdrop, consider creating a standalone panel or wall. Always light your artworks – illumination helps create atmosphere and drama. And, finally, don't clutter a garden with too many pieces, with too many focal points vying for attention. ❞

Sculpture can be challenging to site properly, but when forethought and consideration have been used it can achieve great visual drama – as this dry-stone sphere (and associated imprint within the wall) demonstrate.

Integrity in place

Whereas many pieces of garden art are bought as standalone additions to a garden, some schemes have a much more integrated approach – and Chelsea show gardens are prime examples of this. Their role and purpose are central to the design, bringing together a well-balanced and seamless relationship between planting, hard landscaping, spatial division, practical use and visual appeal. The role of the artwork can be as individual as the garden itself, but the intention should be that without that piece of art your garden would not be as successful as it could be. From wildlife homes to sculptural forms, and vertical finishes to contemporary statements, an integrated approach to artwork and garden-making can create a truly successful outside space.

1

2

DEFINED ROLES

Artwork, whether freestanding or supported, can be as integral to a garden as any other material.

1 Merging artistic and sustainable ideas with practical wildlife use, this vertical 'bug home' incorporates recycled materials, interesting shapes and a quirky overall style.

2 Three arched posts seem to leap out from the informal planting below, and thereby add movement and height to this space.

3 Walls and artwork merge in this unusual design of interconnecting and related circles and hoops, which bring a gratifying sense of flow.

4 These sculptural pineapple cones give focus and a sense of scale to this fine display of clipped topiary forms.

Based on the concept of a plant's cell structure, this garden is an interpretation of a clearing. Form, planting and paving combine artistically and the canopy of pines (*Pinus sylvestris*) gives proportion.

The Times Eureka Garden in association with the Royal Botanic Gardens, Kew, Marcus Barnett, 2011

Personalising space

One of the most fun aspects of garden-making is the personalisation of space, whether in terms of planting combinations, spatial division or how a place is decorated or adorned. The last can be easily and cost effectively achieved in a garden. Often, the placing of a simple sculpture, a combination of elements (such as a group of pots near a water feature) or an actual home-made artefact can be an artistic statement in its own right.

In so doing, the gardener is showing not only a creative side but also staking a visible claim to his/her territory, showing that the space in question belongs or relates to them. And it can be fun! Gardening should be about the personality of the owner coming through, representing unique journeys or historical endeavours. By combining sculpture and art with garden-making, a really personal space can be created.

UNUSUAL TOUCHES

Using local or relevant materials, a personal and specific piece of art can be produced.

1 More than 50 spade heads, new and old, were used to form this substantial sculpture in a garden – for evident reasons – named 'The Ace of Spades'.

2 Charming details such as a stone bead 'necklace' atop a rustic fence can bring bucket-loads of personality and interest to a tiny corner of a garden.

3 In this highly detailed piece of artwork, thousands of different-coloured gravel pieces have been laid in a path leading to a front door, so they recreate scenes from London. As the path is increasingly used, the designer anticipated that the gravel would be moved around and so slowly change the entire pictorial composition.

4 This attractive combination blends historical gardening tools with a contemporary, gridded backing. Together, they make an unusual but personal wall-hung sculpture.

3

EXPERT TIP

Philip Nash
Anchoring sculpture for safety and security

❝ Part of the joy with many pieces of artwork is the apparent 'ease' by which they arise from the ground, so ground fixing is essential. How you secure any piece of artwork in position is dependent on what you have bought or created: its size and material (or materials) will throw up unique challenges and demand specific logistical thought. Generally, though, pots and containers that are to stay in the same location for a long time (that is, not be moved for seasonal display) can be bolted to paving or concrete plinths by drilling a hole through each pot from inside and using a super-strength adhesive to secure it in place. Add weight with ballast to ensure the container really won't move – this not only reduces damage from wind rock but also helps deter any burglars from easily walking out with one of your prized pots. Sculptures (stone or cast pieces, timber or steel) can also be anchored to plinths or concrete pads but do not allow fixing points to be seen; such artworks are best avoided in areas where ball games take place or a high number of visitors may pass. Other products on the market are special anchors and subterranean chains that hold a sculpture in place, without causing visual disruption. If long grass is growing around the base, remember this will need maintaining; strimmers may damage any artwork, so hand cutting of the turf may be necessary. ❞

4

Lightweight home made artworks can be cleverly anchored to a gate or fence relatively easily, but bigger pieces of work will need considerably stronger fixings.

THE M&G GARDEN

Most Chelsea gardens include an element of decoration or adornment within them, but few use sculpture the way leading landscape designer Andy Sturgeon does. He is well known for blurring the boundaries between garden and sculpture, bringing sculptural elements to the core of a design – sometimes creations weave through planting, other times they morph from within or onto an outside building. The result has been a close collaboration between Andy creating outdoors spaces with those sculptors and makers who interpret his brief so well.

At the heart of this garden are two clever but relatively simple techniques – a change in level whereby visitors step down into a space, and an undulating semi-transparent sculpture. Visitors are immediately brought eye-to-eye with the sculpture, thereby encouraging a closer interaction with it. The stepped progress also makes the garden feel bigger than if it was on the flat. The sculpture itself, made from steel rings anodised in copper then polished and waxed, meanders its way through the water, bringing height and movement to the space. The result is a space that feels personal and intimate, while being contemporary in its approach.

WELCOMING SCULPTURE INTO YOUR GARDEN:

- consider its location in the overall scheme – how will it be experienced; will it be fixed to the ground or a wall; will lighting be required to enhance its appeal at night?
- the colour, texture and tone of the artwork (or furniture) should be decided in advance – a deliberate clashing of colours can be successful but requires a keen eye;
- consider using planting to 'hide' some of the sculpture, so there is an element of surprise and delight when people see it;
- you don't have to pay a fortune – a homemade creation has more meaning or purpose, and you can recycle materials;
- there are myriad places to buy off-the-shelf sculpture – flower shows, garden centres, the internet or reclamation yards.

1 Framing the view into the garden is the beautiful *Cercidiphyllum japonicum* (also known as katsura). Its rounded, heart-shaped leaves, which are bronze tinted when young and then fiery yellow/orange in the autumn, cleverly reference the shape of the sculpture.

2 The planting at the front of the garden gives a delicate and detailed composition in contrast to the simpler, greener and more lush planting at the back. Repeating the use of ferns and foliage plants throughout gives a visual consistency to the space.

DESIGNER Andy Sturgeon

CONTRACTOR Creative Landscape Co.

AWARD Gold

CATEGORY Show Garden, 2012

SPONSOR M&G Investments

KEY WORDS levels; water; sculpture; steps; internal walls; sunken

IN A SENTENCE... A calming and majestic way to interplay garden design with contemporary sculpture.

3 The use of Jurassic malt limestone throughout the garden gives visual cohesion. Wide steps lead to a relatively narrow path around the pool – in a real garden it would be recommended to have wider paths around the water to improve access. The stone has been cut smoothly for paving and walls, but the step and water edges left rough giving the scheme interest.

4 To continue the circular theme from the sculpture, different size circles have been cut out of the stone; they are backlit at night. To help reinforce the changing height of the garden, the wall is also split into two levels. This not only creates interest and a sense of adventure in the space, but it helps make the garden feel bigger (and higher) than it actually is.

5 Linking the sculpture to the planting is a subtle task, but immaculately clipped domes of *Ilex crenata* (a small-leaved type of holly) continue the sculpture's rounded and curved theme. More generally, they have been repeated throughout the garden at key points and act as a visual contrast to the straight lines of the steps and walls.

6 At the heart of this design is the 'energy wave' sculpture – made from steel rings anodised in copper then polished and waxed. The transparent nature of it, plus the way it curves inwards and outwards, gives a great sense of movement; underwater lights will ensure it is enjoyed at any time of day or night.

INDEX OF GARDENS AND DESIGNERS

1997 YVES ST LAURENT'S MARRAKECH GARDEN • Designer: Madison Cox **Sponsor:** Yves St Laurent; 18
2000 A CITY SPACE • **Designer:** Mark Anthony Walker **Sponsor:** Cartier Ltd; 18
2001 GARDEN FOR LEARNING • **Designer:** Johnny Woodford, Cleve West; 23
2002 KELLY'S CREEK • **Designer:** Alison Wear, Miranda Melville
2003 THE LACE AND TAPESTRY GARDEN • **Designer:** Kay Yamada **Sponsor:** Barakura English Garden; 22
GARDEN FROM THE DESERT • **Designer:** Christopher Bradley-Hole **Sponsor:** His Highness Sheikh Zayed Bin Sultan al-Nahyan; 19

SHOW GARDENS 2004
THE MERRILL LYNCH GARDEN • **Designer:** Dan Pearson Studio **Sponsor:** Merrill Lynch
HORTUS CONCLUSUS • **Designer:** Christopher Bradley-Hole **Sponsor:** His Highness Shaikh Zayed Bin Sultan Al-Nahyan
LAURENT-PERRIER HARPERS & QUEEN GARDEN • **Designer:** Terence Conran, Nicola Lesbirel **Sponsors:** Laurent-Perrier, Harpers & Queen
THE SALVATION ARMY & BUILDBASE GARDEN – 'FROM DARKNESS TO LIGHT' • **Designer:** Julian Dowle (Julian Dowle Partnership) **Sponsor:** Buildbase
THE STONEMARKET BOAT RACE ANNIVERSARY GARDEN • **Designer:** Bunny Guinness **Sponsor:** Stonemarket
THE NATIONAL LOTTERY GARDEN – 'A COLOURFUL SUBURBAN EDEN' • **Designer:** Diarmuid Gavin **Sponsor:** The National Lottery
THE KNIGHTSBRIDGE URBAN RENAISSANCE GARDEN • **Designer:** Phil Jaffa (Scape Design Associates) in association with Patrick Collins **Sponsor:** The Knightsbridge Development; 120 (b); 194 (l)
LIFE GARDEN • **Designer:** Jane Hudson, Erik De Maeijer **Sponsor:** Thompson Landscapes; 124 (tl), 196 (cl)
THE HADDONSTONE KNOT GARDEN • **Designer:** Simon Scott **Sponsor:** Haddonstone Ltd
FLEMINGS NURSERIES AUSTRALIAN INSPIRATION • **Designer:** Jim Fogarty (Jim Fogarty Design Pty Ltd) **Sponsor:** Flemings Nurseries
THE DAIHATSU GREEN GARDEN • **Designer:** The Burntwood School **Sponsor:** Daihatsu Cars
WILLIAM TURNER GARDEN • **Designers:** Casella Stanger, Chris Davis **Sponsors:** Northumberland Strategic Partnership, Morpeth Town Council, Heritage Lottery Fund, Casella Stanger, Hellens
THE GARDMAN WILD BIRD GARDEN • **Designer:** David Domoney **Sponsor:** Gardman Ltd
100% PURE NEW ZEALAND ORA – GARDEN OF WELL-BEING • **Designers:** Kim Jarrett, Trish Waugh, Lyonel Grant, Doug Waugh, Tina Hart, Brian Massey **Sponsor:** Tourism New Zealand
THE PAVESTONE GARDEN • **Designer:** Geoffrey Whiten **Sponsor:** Pavestone (UK) Ltd in association with Essential Water Garden Magazine; 42 (b)
THE 4HEAD GARDEN – FROM MERLIN TO MEDICINE • **Designer:** Marney Hall, **Sponsor:** 4head
THE PLANT HUNTERS • **Designers:** Mike Baldwin, Gill Thomas **Sponsor:** Bradstone
FROM FREEDOM TO FUTURE • **Designer:** Park & Countryside Landscape Architects (Leeds City Council) **Sponsor:** Leeds City Council, with assistance from Thorpe Park Leeds and Munro K
THE JAPANESE WAY • **Designer:** Maureen Busby Garden Designs **Sponsors:** CED, Herons Bonsai, Coblands, Travis Perkins
HOPE • **Designers:** Staff and prisoners from HMP Leyhill **Sponsor:** Gem Horticulture
THE WOOLWORTHS GARDEN • **Designers:** Graduates from The Pickard School of Garden Design **Sponsor:** Woolworths

SHOW GARDENS 2005
MERRILL LYNCH GARDEN • **Designer:** Andy Sturgeon (Andy Sturgeon Garden Design) **Sponsor:** Merrill Lynch; 108; 139 (t); 210-211
IN THE GROVE • **Designer:** Christopher Bradley-Hole **Sponsor:** His late Highness Shaikh Zayed bin Sultan Al-Nahyan; 148-149
LAURENT-PERRIER GARDEN • **Designer:** Tom Stuart-Smith Landscape Design **Sponsors:** Laurent-Perrier (UK) Ltd, Trentham Leisure Ltd; 73 (bl)
THE ECOVER CHELSEA PENSIONERS' GARDEN • **Designer:**

Julian Dowle (Julian Dowle Partnership) **Sponsor:** Ecover
THE PEACE GARDEN • **Designer:** Sir Terence Conran (Conran & Partners) **Sponsor:** Big Lottery Fund; 99 (l)
HANOVER QUAY GARDEN • **Designer:** Diarmuid Gavin **Sponsors:** Park Developments Ltd and John Sisk & Son Ltd, Marshalls, Westland Horticulture, Unwins Seeds, Marian Finucane Show; 95 (cr)
THE TRAILFINDERS RECYCLED GARDEN • **Designer:** Chris Beardshaw Ltd **Sponsor:** Trailfinders; 128-129; 142 (r)
THE FETZER WINE GARDEN • **Designer:** Kate Frey **Sponsor:** Brown-Forman Wines; 69 (bl); 112
THE CANCER RESEARCH UK GARDEN • **Designers:** Jane Hudson and Erik De Maeijer **Sponsor:** Private donor; 31 (b); 117 (tl)
FLEMING'S NURSERIES FLOAT • **Designer:** Jack Merlo (Jack Merlo Design) **Sponsor:** Fleming's Nurseries; 52 (b); 107 (tr)
BOREAL FOREST GARDEN • **Designer:** Landlab **Sponsors:** Taiga Rescue Network, Lorberg Baumschulerzeugnisse, United Utilities, Laurieston Hall Community, Landlab; 161 (tr and br)
MOAT & CASTLE ECO-GARDEN • **Designers:** Ellen Mary Fenton & Neil Malachy Black **Sponsor:** National Savings and Investments
SAVILLS GARDEN: THE GRAND TOUR • **Designer:** Clare Agnew **Sponsor:** Savills in association with After the Antique; 109 (br)
THE 4HEAD GARDEN • **Designer:** Marney Hall **Sponsor:** 4head; 117 (tr)
BRADSTONE SPRING GARDEN • **Designer:** Alan Sargent **Sponsor:** Bradstone
THE WILDLIFE TRUSTS LUSH GARDEN • **Designer:** Stephen Hall **Sponsor:** Lush UK; 97 (tr); 166 (tl)
THE REAL RUBBISH GARDEN • **Designer:** Claire Whitehouse **Sponsor:** SITA Environmental Trust; 114-115; 146
THE FISHERMAN'S GARDEN • **Designers:** Geoffrey Whiten, Josh Whiten **Sponsor:** Pavestone; 114-115; 146
THE SPIRAL GARDEN • **Designer:** Carol Smith **Sponsors:** M&M Timber, Marshalls, Osmose, Steve Cooper, Sugarbrook Nurseries, Colin Smith Electrical, AC Electrical, Buildbase, Topglass, University of Gloucestershire, Worcester Aquatics
CHIC GARDENS THE GALLERY OUTSIDE • **Designer:** Philip Nixon, Marcus Barnett; 147 (br)
THE ROALD DAHL FOUNDATION CHOCOLATE GARDEN • **Designer:** Landscape Management Services / Home Group **Sponsors:** Home Group, Warner Bros; 142 (l)
COURTYARD GARDENS THE PHILOSOPHER'S GARDEN • **Designer:** Andrew Loudon **Sponsor:** SWS UK Ltd; 209 (r)
THE CUMBRIAN FELLSIDE GARDEN • **Designer:** Kim Wilde, Richard Lucas **Sponsors:** Wyevale Garden Centres plc, The World of Beatrix Potter, Cumbria Tourist Board, Holker Hall and Gardens; 215
SIMON'S GARDEN WITH VA VA VROOM • **Designer:** Scenic Blue Design Team; 147 (tr); 118 (tr)
CITY GARDEN REFLECTIONS • **Designer:** David Domoney **Sponsor:** The Sunday Mirror; 62-63; 133 (tr)

SHOW GARDENS 2006
SAGA INSURANCE GARDEN • **Designer:** Cleve West **Sponsor:** Saga Insurance; 111 (b)
THE SAVILLS GARDEN • **Designers:** Marcus Barnett, Philip Nixon **Sponsor:** Savills plc; 34-35; 61 (tl); 77 (tl); 207 (b); 53 (tr)
LAURENT-PERRIER GARDEN • **Designer:** Jinny Blom (Jinny Blom Ltd) **Sponsor:** Laurent-Perrier (UK) Ltd; 56 (tl)
THE DAILY TELEGRAPH GARDEN • **Designer:** Tom Stuart-Smith **Sponsor:** The Daily Telegraph; 52-53; 111 (tr); 38 (br); 70
THE 100% PURE NEW ZEALAND GARDEN • **Designer:** Xanthe White **Sponsor:** Tourism New Zealand supported by Air New Zealand, Tourism Auckland, Tailor Made Travel, Titan HiTours; 7 (l); 105 (b); 121; 124 (bl); 205 (c); 209 (l)
WALKING BAREFOOT WITH BRADSTONE • **Designer:** Sarah Eberle in collaboration with Andrew Herring **Sponsor:** Bradstone; 48-49; 89 (tr)
BARNSLEY HOUSE SPA GARDEN • **Designer:** Stephen Woodhams (Woodhams Ltd) **Sponsor:** Barnsley House; 8-9
THE CANCER RESEARCH UK GARDEN • **Designer:** Andy Sturgeon **Sponsor:** Private donor; 117 (b), 94
THE 4HEAD GARDEN OF DREAMS • **Designers:** Marney Hall, Heather Yarrow **Sponsor:** 4head; 117 (b)
RAVINE GARDEN: GIFT OF THE GLACIER • **Designer:** Catharina Malmberg-Snodgrass (CMS Design Associates) **Sponsor:** Lake Forest Garden Club
FLEMING'S NURSERIES AUSTRALIAN GARDEN PRESENTED BY TRAILFINDERS • **Designer:** Dean Herald

Sponsors: Fleming's Nurseries, Trailfinders; 90 (br); 100-101; 124 (tr); 133 (b)
THE HALIFAX GARDEN – 'THESE FOUR WALLS' • **Designer:** Stuart Perry Consultants **Sponsor:** Halifax plc; 17; 91 (l); 120 (tl); 122-123
THE ROCKWOOL GARDEN ROOM • **Designer:** Barry Mayled **Sponsor:** Rockwool Ltd
LEEDS CITY COUNCIL GARDEN • **Designer:** Leeds City Council – Parks & Countryside Service **Sponsor:** Munroe K
GARDENAFRICA • **Designer:** Alan Capper (Kent Design) in partnership with Ross Allan Designs **Sponsor:** UK based charitable trusts; 6 (bl)
THE PAVESTONE GARDEN (A Garden of Tranquillity) • **Designer:** Geoffrey Whiten **Sponsor:** Pavestone UK Ltd
THE CHRIS BEARDSHAW WORMCAST GARDEN – 'GROWING FOR LIFE' AT BOVERIDGE HOUSE • **Designer:** Chris Beardshaw **Sponsor:** The Wormcast Company Ltd
THE JURASSIC COAST GARDEN • **Designer:** Nick Williams-Ellis **Sponsors:** Jurassic Coast Dorset & East Devon Heritage Site, Minster Joinery, Landers Quarries
GORILLA GARDEN • **Designer:** Graham Pockett **Sponsor:** Zoological Society of London; 95 (cl)
CITY GARDEN THE MENCAP & CATER ALLEN BANK GARDEN • **Designer:** Ruth Marshall; 196 (r)

SHOW GARDENS 2007
THE AMNESTY INTERNATIONAL GARDEN FOR HUMAN RIGHTS • **Designers:** Paula Ryan, Artillery Architecture & Interior Design; 67 (b)
LLOYDS TSB GARDEN • **Designer:** Trevor Tooth **Sponsor:** Lloyds TSB
THE FETZER SUSTAINABLE WINERY GARDEN • **Designer:** Kate Frey **Sponsor:** Fetzer Vineyards; 164 (b)
SCENT OF A ROMAN • **Designer:** Leeds City Council – Parks & Countryside Service **Sponsors:** Thorpe Park Developments Ltd, Haddonstone Ltd
THE MARSHALL'S SUSTAINABILITY GARDEN • **Designer:** Scenic Blue Design Team **Sponsor:** Marshalls plc; 135 (b); 141 (r); 170-171
THE SAVILLS GARDEN • **Designer:** Marcus Barnett, Philip Nixon **Sponsor:** Savills plc; 109 (t)
LAURENT-PERRIER GARDEN • **Designer:** Jinny Blom (Jinny Blom Ltd) **Sponsor:** Laurent-Perrier (UK) Ltd; 46-47
THE DAILY TELEGRAPH GARDEN • **Designers:** Isabelle Van Groeningen, Gabriella Pape, artist Simon Packard **Sponsor:** Telegraph Media Group; 51; 76-77; 208 (tl)
THE CHRIS BEARDSHAW GARDEN IN ASSOCIATION WITH BUILDBASE • **Designer:** Chris Beardshaw **Sponsor:** Buildbase; 96 (t); 184 (l)
CANCER RESEARCH UK GARDEN • **Designer:** Andy Sturgeon Garden Design; 94 (t and br); 150-151
THE FORTNUM & MASON GARDEN • **Designer:** Robert Myers Associates **Sponsor:** Fortnum & Mason; 71 (b); 74 (tc); 119 (t); 160-61 (b)
600 DAYS WITH BRADSTONE • **Designer:** Sarah Eberle **Sponsor:** Bradstone; 6 (cl); 43 (r); 72 (bl); 90 (b); 116 (br); 136 (b); 169 (t)
THE WESTLAND GARDEN • **Designers:** Diarmuid Gavin, Stephen Reilly **Sponsor:** Westland Horticulture Ltd; 82-83; 85 (c); 97 (b)
A TRIBUTE TO LINNAEUS • **Designer:** Ulf Nordfjell (Stockholm) **Sponsors:** The National Linnaeus Tercentenary Committee (Stockholm), Axel & Margaret Ax: son Johnson Foundation, The Bank of Sweden Tercentenary Foundation, The Sten A Olsson Foundation for Research & Culture; 12 (b); 45 (l); 54 (t); 139 (b); 143 (l)
FLEMING'S & TRAILFINDERS AUSTRALIAN GARDEN • **Designer:** Mark Browning (Cycas Landscape Design) **Sponsors:** Fleming's Nurseries, Trailfinders
THROUGH THE MOONGATE • **Designer:** Lesley Bremness (East West Garden Design), **Sponsors:** Royal Bank of Scotland Group, Bank of China; 45 (b); 85 (cr); 112 (inset)
THE THOMAS TELFORD TOLL HOUSE GARDEN • **Designers:** Michael Vout, Chris Jones **Sponsors:** Ironbridge Gorge Museum Trust, Harper Adams University College, P&W Maintenance Contracting Ltd, British Wildflower Plants, Telford & Wrekin Services Ltd, Dingle Nurseries, Shropshire Stone & Granite Ltd, Banbury Innovations – GRP products, Craven Dunnill Jackfield Ltd, Wellington Town Partnership
THE BRETT LANDSCAPING GARDEN – RELATIONSHIPS • **Designer:** Geoffrey Whiten **Sponsor:** Brett Landscaping and Building Products
THE HASMEAD SAND & ICE GARDEN • **Designer:** Linda Bush **Sponsor:** Hasmead plc; 141 (t)
CHETWOODS GARDEN • **Designer:** Laurie Chetwood, Patrick Collins, 194 (r)
CHIC GARDEN THE CHILDREN'S SOCIETY LUST FOR LIFE

GARDEN • Designer: Angus Thompson; 116 (tr)
CITY GARDEN A CITY HAVEN COURTYARD • Designer: Harpak design; 14-15; 124 (br)
REALISTIC RETREAT • Designer: Adam Frost; 73 (bl);125 (l)
COURTYARD GARDEN CAF GIVING GARDEN 'WHERE THE WILD THINGS ARE' • Designer: Tiggy Salt, Green Ink Gardens Ltd; 20
THE OLD GATE • Designer: Adam Woolcott, Jonathan Smith Sponsors: Croudace Homes, Langthorns Plantery, Cox's Architectural Salvage; 154-155; 176-177
TUFA TEA • Designer: Kati Crome; 91 (b)
SHINGLESEA • Designer: Chris O'Donoghue Sponsor: Robert Patch Furniture, 1066 Country, Merriments Gardens, Travis Perkins, John Jempson & Son; 44 (l); 69 (t); 155 (t); 214 (r)
CAPEL MANOR COLLEGE, CAPEL MANOR DESIGN • 205 (br)
CONTINUOUS LEARNING • Writtle College; 158 (t)
CLAPTON PARK PARK MANAGEMENT ORGANISATION/ GRASS ROOF COMPANY • 164 (t)
KIRSTENBOSCH • 140 (l)

SHOW GARDENS 2008
ELEVATIONS • Designer: Philip Nash (Philip Nash Designs) Sponsor: Gavin Jones Ltd, Dupont™ Corian ®, Philip Nash Design Ltd; 58-59; 50 (br); 110 (l)
SUMMER SOLSTICE • Designers: del Buono Gazerwitz, Spencer Fung Architects; Sponsor: Daylesford Organic; 68 (r); 186-187
OCEAN TO A GARDEN • Designer: Paul Cooper Sponsors: Testi Fratelli srl, H2O plc
THE LARGEST ROOM IN THE HOUSE • Designer: Denise Preston Sponsors:GMI Property Company Ltd, The Royal British Legion, Toc H; 04 (c); 87 (b)
THE MARSHALLS GARDEN THAT KIDS REALLY WANT! • Designers: Marshalls Gardens & Driveways, Ian Dexter Sponsor: Marshalls plc; 95 (b); 137 (t); 33
THE BUPA GARDEN • Designer: Cleve West Sponsor: Bupa; 64-65; 54 (c)
I DREAM, I SEEK MY GARDEN • Designer: Shao Fan Sponsors: KT Wong Charitable Trust, De Beers; 13
THE SAVILLS GARDEN • Designer: Philip Nixon Sponsor: Savills plc; 54 (r); 94 (bl); 216-217
THE DAILY TELEGRAPH GARDEN • Designer: Arabella Lennox-Boyd Sponsor: The Daily Telegraph; 126-127
THE LAURENT-PERRIER GARDEN • Designer: Tom Stuart-Smith; 39;78-79; 147 (tl)
CANCER RESEARCH UK GARDEN • Designer: Andy Sturgeon Garden Design Ltd; 2;135 (t)
THE LLOYDS TSB GARDEN • Designer: Trevor Tooth; 38 (c); 40-41; 55 (l); 69 (tr); 120 (r);139 (cl)
A CADOGAN GARDEN • Designer: Robert Myers Sponsor: Cadogan Estates Ltd; 12 (t); 32 (c); 39 (b and tr); 60; 82 (b)
THE OCEÂNICO GARDEN • Designers: Diarmuid Gavin, Sir Terence Conran Sponsor: The Oceânico Group; 31 (tr); 43 (l); 66-67; 198-199; 200-201
FROM LIFE TO LIFE, A GARDEN FOR GEORGE • Designer: Yvonne Innes Sponsors: The Material World Charitable Foundation, Harrisongs Ltd; 140 (r);212-213
FLEMING'S & TRAILFINDERS AUSTRALIAN GARDEN presented by Melbourne, Victoria • Designer: Jamie Durie (Patio Landscape Architecture & Design) Sponsors: Fleming's Nurseries, Trailfinders; 92-93; 117 (cr); 136 (l)
THE QVC GARDEN • Designer: Wynniatt-Husey Clarke Ltd Sponsor: QVC; 32 (bl); 33 (l); 71 (tr)
THE REFLECTIVE GARDEN • Designer: Clare Agnew Design Sponsor: Ruffer LLP; 39 (tl); 85 (b)
NORTH EAST ENGLAND @ HOME GARDEN • Designers: Penny Denoon, John Carmichael Sponsors: Home Group Ltd, One NorthEast; 180 (l)
REAL LIFE BY BRETT • Designer: Geoff Whiten Sponsors: Brett Landscaping and Building Products; 74 (tl); 96 (b); 118 (r)
GARDEN IN THE SILVER MOONLIGHT • Designers: Haruko Seki, Makoto Saito (add.locus architects) Sponsors: Royal Palm Residences Seychelles, Urban Regenerate Association of Niigata, The Great Britain Sasakawa Foundation; 109 (b) Designer: Gabriel Ash; 176 (b)
URBAN GARDEN THE SKY AT NIGHT • Designer: Barry Mayled (Homes & Gardens Ltd.) Sponsors: Acorn Gardens, Euroclad Ltd., Hopkins Law LLP, Eurobond Ltd, Dudley's Ltd; 85 (t)
MIDORINO TOBIRA – THE GREEN DOOR • Designer: Kazuyuki Ishihara Sponsor: Oshhima Shipbuilding Group, AOA Corporation Ltd; 45 (r)
THE LK BENNETT GARDEN • Designer: Rachel de Thame; 56 (b) (l); 133 (br)
THE CHILDREN'S SOCIETY GARDEN • Designer: Mark

Gregory; 138 (b); 166 (tr)
THE PEMBERTON GREENISH RECESS GARDEN • Designer: Paul Hensey with Knoll Gardens Sponsor: Pemberton Greenish; 26 (b); 33 (b); 53 (b); 91 (r; 124 (tr); 132-133
TEMPEST IN A TEAPOT • Designer: Thomas Hoblyn Garden Design Ltd Sponsor: Foreign & Colonial Investment Trust; 32 (r);111 (tl)
COURTYARD GARDEN THE DORSET CEREALS EDIBLE PLAYGROUND • Designer: Nick Williams; 181 (l); 182 (l) 183 r; 184 (b)
THE SIMMONS & SIMMONS GARDEN: A JOURNEY TO WORK • Designer: Growing Ambition Sponsors: Simmons & Simmons; 97 (tl)
SPANA'S COURTYARD GARDEN • Designer: Chris O'Donoghue Sponsor: SPANA 83 (t)
THE SHETLAND CROFT HOUSE GARDEN • Designer: Sue Hayward Sponsors: Motor Neurone Disease; 111 (bl)
SAIL FOR GOLD • Hilliers; 96 (tr)
CHRISTOPHER LISNEY • Garden Sculpture; 208 (cr)

SHOW GARDENS 2009
THE CANARY ISLANDS SPA GARDEN • Designers: David Cubero & James Wong Sponsor: Canary Islands Tourist Board; 81 (t); 59 (bc)
ECHOES OF JAPAN IN AN ENGLISH GARDEN • Designer: Kay Yamada Sponsors: Barakura English Garden, TV Kanagawa Inc, Asahi Breweries Ltd, All Nippon Airways Co Ltd, Daikanen; 105 (t); 195 (cr)
THE QVC GARDEN • Designer: Adam Frost Sponsors: QVC; 125 (t)
FUTURE NATURE • Designers: Adrian Hallam, Chris Arrowsmith, Nigel Dunnett Sponsors: Yorkshire Water, University of Sheffield Alumni Fund, Green City Initiative, Buro Happold; 21; 68 (l); 159; 165 (r); 172-173; 210 (l)
THE MARSHALLS LIVING STREET • Designer: Ian Dexter (Marshalls) Sponsor: Marshalls plc; 26 (t); 36 (r); 15 (bl); 157 (bl); 167 (b)
THE FOREIGN & COLONIAL INVESTMENT'S GARDEN • Designer: Thomas Hoblyn Sponsor: Foreign & Colonial Investment Trust; 106-107 (t); 113 (b)
THE DAILY TELEGRAPH GARDEN • Designer: Ulf Nordfjell Sponsor: The Daily Telegraph; 16; 61 (bl); 66 (l); 67 (t);74 (br); 83 (b)
THE LAURENT-PERRIER GARDEN • Designer: Luciano Giubbilei Sponsor: Champagne Laurent-Perrier; 24-25; 63 (r); 129 (l); 196 (b)
THE CANCER RESEARCH UK GARDEN • Designer: Robert Myers Sponsor: Cancer Research UK; 27; 119 (b); 211 (t)
THE KEY • Designer: Paul Stone Sponsors: Homes and Communities Agency, Communities and Local Government, London Employer Accord; 165 (l and br); 167 (tl); 203 (t)
THE HESCO GARDEN • Designer: Leeds City Council Sponsor: HESCO Bastion Ltd; 113 (tl); 154 (bl); 177 (r)
THE QUILTED VELVET GARDEN • Designer: Tony Smith Sponsor: Quilted Velvet; 90 (lm)
PERFUME GARDEN • Designers: Laurie Chetwood & Patrick Collins Sponsors: Gazeley, P&G Prestige Products and Chetwoods Architects
URBAN GARDENS THE WITAN WISDOM GARDEN • Designer: Nicholas Dexter; Sponsor: Witan Investment Trust; 37 (b); 136-137
ECO CHIC • Designers: Kate Gould • Sponsor: Helios; 88 (r); 102-103; 143 (r); 28 (c); 37 (f)
THE CHILDREN'S SOCIETY GARDEN • Designer: Mark Gregory; 98 (tl and br); 118 (b); 179 (bl); 184 (r); 188; 192 (tl); 195 (tl)
CREDIT CRUNCH: THE OVERDRAWN ARTIST'S GARDEN • Designer: Sarah Eberle; 215 (t and bl)
CREDIT CRUNCH: THE OFF-SHORE GARDEN • Designer: Sarah Eberle; 44 (r)
CREDIT CRUNCH: THE BANKER'SGARDEN • Designer: Sarah Eberle; 206
NATURE ASCENDING • Designers: Jane Broadbank, Angus Thompson; 10-11 (tc); 29 (b);157 (t); 161 (tl and cl);162-163
1984 • Designer: Anthony Cox, Chris Gutteridge, Jon Owens; 158 (b); 208 (b)
THE PSI NURSERY GARDEN • Designer: Jamie Dunstan Sponsor: PSI Nursery; 50 (b); 95 (t)
THE FENCHURCH GARDEN • Designer: Paul Hensey Sponsors: Fenchurch Advisory Partners;28-29;133 (a)157(br)
THE MODERN ROCK GARDEN • Designer: Tomoko Osonoe Sponsor: Tecnoplan Co Ltd; 31 (l); 72 (t)
A JAPANESE TRANQUIL RETREAT • Designer: Takumi Awai; 199 (b)
THE ACE OF SPADES • Designer: David Domoney; 98 (tr); 165 (tr); 214 (l);
COURTYARD GARDEN TIME TO THINK, SPACE TO BREATHE

• Designers: Tony Davy, Mike Roberts, Warwickshire College; 166 (r)
FENLAND ALCHEMIST GARDEN • Designers: Jane Besser, Stephen Hall; 21
POTTERING IN NORTH CUMBRIA • Designers: Stephen Hall, Jane Besset; 160 (t)
DEMELZA • Designer: Jo Thompson; 156
FRESHLY PREPARED BY ARALIA • Designer: Patrica Fox (Aralia Garden Design); Sponsors: Pawley & Malyon, Heather Barnes, Attwater & Liell; 184 (t); 185 (l); 182 (c)
GENERATION GARDENS RANELAGH SCHOOL LEARNING TO GROW • Designers: Mary Payne, Jon Wheatley in partnership with Ranelagh School; 178
THE WIDOW'S GARDEN • Garden Design Centre at Scotsdale; 42 (t)
OTHER THE SCULPTURE PARK, Jumps Road, Churt, Farnham, Surrey; 206
ARCHITECTURAL HERITAGE, Horse of the Moon Artist: Nic Fiddian Green; 207
MARSTON AND LANZINGER 176; 182-183
A PLANTSMAN'S PALETTE' Roger Platts Garden Design and Nurseries; 56 (r); 62 (t); 84 (t)
THOMPSON'S GALLERY, (in association with Janet Macleod); 205 (t)

SHOW GARDENS 2010
THE CHILDREN'S SOCIETY Garden Designer: Mark Gregory
THE L'OCCITANE GARDEN Designer: James Towillis Sponsor: L'Occitane
THE VICTORIAN AVIARY GARDEN – SOUTH LAKES HOTELS Designer: Jonathan Denby, Philippa Pearson Sponsor: South Lakes Hotels, Kirkstone
KAZAHANA (A LIGHT SNOW FLURRY FROM A CLOUDLESS SKY) Designer: Kazuyuki Ishihara Sponsors: Yuraka Co Ltd, Virgin Atlantic Airways Ltd, Fuji Kogyo Co Ltd, Toho-Leo Ltd, Kanehon Co Ltd, Higashi Nihon House Co Ltd
THE M&G GARDEN DESIGNER: Roger Platts; Sponsor: M&G Investments
KEBONY – NATURALLY NORWAY Designer: Darren Saines Sponsors: Kebony, Darren Saines Garden Design, The Norwegian Embassy, Innovation Norway, Lorberg, Lundhs, Durisol
LAURENT-PERRIER GARDEN Designer: Tom Stuart-Smith Sponsor: Laurent-Perrier
THE DAILY TELEGRAPH GARDEN Designer: Andy Sturgeon Sponsor: The Daily Telegraph
THE CANCER RESEARCH UK GARDEN Designer: Robert Myers
THE HESCO GARDEN 2010 Designer: Leeds City Council Sponsor: HESCO Bastion Ltd
FOREIGN & COLONIAL INVESTMENTS' GARDEN Designer: Thomas Hoblyn Sponsor: Foreign & Colonial Investment
THE TOURISM MALAYSIA GARDEN Designer: David Cubero & James Wong (Amphibian Designs Ltd) Sponsor: Tourism Malaysia
TRAILFINDERS AUSTRALIAN GARDEN presented by Fleming's Designer: Scott Wynd Sponsors: Trailfinders, Fleming's Nurseries
THE STEPHEN HAWKING GARDEN FOR MOTOR NEURONE DISEASE Designer: Sue Hayward Sponsor: Brewin Dolphin Ltd
PLACES OF CHANGE Designer: Paul Stone in partnership with Roderick James Architects LLP, Jane Knight, Architecture sans Frontières-UK, BCHA (Bournemouth), Crisis Skylight (London), Look Ahead (London), Noah Enterprises (Luton), Providence Row (London), Supported Housing for Young People – SHYPP (Ross-on-Wye), Stonham (Hull & Maidstone) Sponsors: Homes & Communities Agency, Communities & Local Government, London Employer Accord
URBAN GARDENS
THE WATERLESS WATER GARDEN Designers: Tomoko Osonoe, Kei Iwata
ACE OF DIAMONDS Designer: David Domoney Sponsor: bmi Diamond Club
THE JOHN JOSEPH MECHI GARDEN Designer: Benjamin Wincott (Writtle College) Sponsor: Wilkin & Sons (Tiptree); 45 (tr), 55
A JOY FOREVER Designer: Kate Gould (Kate Gould Gardens) Sponsor: Hartman UK; 911
THE NATURALLY FASHIONABLE GARDEN Designer: NDG+ Sponsor: BrandAlley; 85 (t)
THE UNIVERSITY OF WORCESTER GARDEN Designer: Olivia Kirk (KKE Architects Ltd) Sponsor: The University of Worcester supported by Buildbase Ltd; 72(r); 141(l)
DYSLEXIA – A BARRIER TO EDUCATION? Designer: Tim Fowler Garden Design Sponsors: The Driver Youth Trust, M Malkmas, J Stein; 42 (t)

BRADSTONE BIODIVERSITY GARDEN Designer: Paul Harvey-Brookes (Chris Beardshaw Scholar 2009) Sponsor: Chris Beardshaw Mentoring Scholarship sponsored by Bradstone

THE EASIGRASS GARDEN (THE URBAN PLANTAHOLIC'S KITCHEN GARDEN) Designer: Tony Smith Sponsor: Easigrass

GROWING WORLD CLASS TALENT Designer: Paul Green (The Green Design Partnership) Sponsors: Askham Bryan College, Association of Plumbing & Heating Contractors (APHC), Bulldog Tools, Darren Thompson Joinery, Gadd Brothers, Jewson, Keith Chapman Landscapes, Makita, Marshalls, National Wildflower Centre, Tarmac, Trad-lite, York Survey & Supply Centre, Woodkirk Stone; 38 (bl)

THE UNEXPECTED GARDENER Designer: Jo Thompson

THE GO MODERN GARDEN Designer: Jamie Dunstan (Gardeners' Boutique) Sponsor: Go Modern

COURTYARD GARDENS

LIGHTS & COLOURS OF THE ALPS Designers: Francesco Decembrini, Daniele Zanzi

WELCOME TO YORKSHIRE'S RHUBARB CRUMBLE & CUSTARD GARDEN Designer: Gillespies LLP Sponsor: Welcome to Yorkshire

A CENTENARY GARDEN FOR CAPTAIN R F SCOTT Designer: Cardiff Council Parks Service in conjunction with Celf Creative Sponsors: Dean & Dyball Civil Engineering, Cardiff Marine Group

THE PINE & CONIFER ENTHUSIAST GARDEN Designer: Graham Bodle

MUSIC ON THE MOORS Designer: Christina Williams Sponsors: Dartmoor & Exmoor National Parks Sustainable Development Funds, Rathbones

SAC STRUTT & PARKER SUSTAINABLE HIGHLAND GARDEN Designer: Amber Goudy Sponsors: Strutt & Parker, SAC

CHRISTIAN BEFORE DIOR Designers: Patricia Thirion, Janet Honour Sponsor: Chilstone of Tunbridge Wells

GLOBAL STONE BEE FRIENDLY PLANTS GARDEN Designers: Janey Auchincloss, Paul Hammond Sponsor: Global Stone (Colchester) Ltd

GREEN & BLACK'S RAINFOREST GARDEN Designer: Jane Owen with Ann-Marie Powell Sponsor: Green & Black's

GENERATION GARDENS

THE UPWARDLY MOBILE GARDEN Designer: Chris Deakin, Jason Lock Sponsors: John Woods Nurseries, Capel Manor College, The Sun Newspaper, Urbis Design, Marshalls

MORRISONS LET'S GROW TO CHELSEA GARDEN Designers: The Garden Design Centre, The Sun Newspaper Sponsors: Morrisons, The Sun Newspaper

A CITY ROOF GARDEN Designers: Geoff & Kas Whiten Sponsors: Digby Stone Ltd, Folia (Europe) Ltd, BG Building Contractors, The Sun Newspaper

THE SUN GOLDEN WEDDING GARDEN Designer: Val Christman (Class Gardens) Sponsor: The Sun Newspaper

SHOW GARDENS 2011

The HESCO Garden Designer: Leeds City Council Sponsor: HESCO Bastion Ltd

BRITISH HEART FOUNDATION GARDEN Designer: Ann-Marie Powell Sponsor: Brewin Dolphin

THE SKYSHADES GARDEN – POWERED BY LIGHT Designer: Marney Hall Sponsor: SKYShades UK Ltd

RBC NEW WILD GARDEN Designer: Nigel Dunnett & The Landscape Agency Sponsor: Royal Bank of Canada

THE M&G GARDEN Designer: Bunny Guinness Sponsor: M&G Investments

A MONACO GARDEN Designer: Sarah Eberle Sponsor: Principality of Monaco

THE AUSTRALIAN GARDEN PRESENTED BY THE ROYAL BOTANIC GARDENS MELBOURNE Designer: Jim Fogarty Sponsors: State Government of Victoria, Macquarie Group, Tourism Victoria, Maxwell & Williams, City of Casey, R.M.Williams

LAURENT-PERRIER GARDEN BY LUCIANO GIUBBILEI – NATURE & HUMAN INTERVENTION Designer: Luciano Giubbilei Sponsor: Laurent-Perrier

THE DAILY TELEGRAPH GARDEN Designer: Cleve West Sponsor: The Daily Telegraph

THE CANCER RESEARCH UK GARDEN Designer: Robert Myers Sponsor: Cancer Research UK

THE TIME EUREKA GARDEN IN ASSOCIATION WITH THE ROYAL BOTANIC GARDENS, KEW Designer: Marcus Barnett Sponsor: The Times

TOURISM MALAYSIA GARDEN Designer: David Cubero & James Wong (Amphibian Designs) Sponsor: Tourism Malaysia

IRISH SKY GARDEN Designer: Diarmuid Gavin Sponsors: Fáilte Ireland, Cork City Council

THE HOMEBASE CORNISH MEMORIES GARDEN Designer: Thomas Hoblyn Sponsor: Homebase

TRAILFINDERS AUSTRALIAN GARDEN PRESENTED BY FLEMING'S Designer: Ian Barker (Ian Barker Garden Design) Sponsors: Trailfinders, Fleming's Nurseries

A BEAUTIFUL PARADISE (MAKING MEMORIES WITH A GREEN POEM) Designer: Kazuyuki Ishihara Sponsors: Kazuyuki Ishihara Design Laboratory co Ltd, HB-101, Rakuen Town, Karino Japan, Kubiki Co Ltd, Jyutaro, Virgin Atlantic Airways Ltd, Cats Co Ltd, Majestic Trees, Mokichi Landscape, Nitori

THE B&Q GARDEN Designers: Laurie Chetwood & Patrick Collins (Chetwoods)

URBAN GARDENS

THE LAND'S END ACROSS THE POND GARDEN Designer: Adam Frost Sponsor: Land's End

WINDS OF CHANGE Designer: Jamie Dunstan (Gardener's Boutique) Sponsor: Stockton Drilling Ltd

THE CHILSTONE GARDEN Designer: Heather Appleton Sponsor: Chilstone of Tunbridge Wells

THE POWER OF NATURE Designer: Olivia Kirk (KKE Architects) Sponsor: Worcester, Bosch Group

THE MAGISTRATE'S GARDEN Designer: Kate Gould (Kate Gould Gardens) Sponsor: The Magistrate's Association

DONCASTER DEAF TRUST GARDEN Designer: Graham Bodle

THE BRADSTONE FUSION GARDEN Designer: The Chris Beardshaw Mentoring Scholarship Team Sponsor: Bradstone

RNIB GARDEN Designer: Paul Harvey-Brookes Sponsor: Royal National Institute of Blind People

ARTISAN GARDENS

A CHILD'S GARDEN IN WALES Designers: Ysgol Bryn Castell & Heronsbridge School Horticulture Students with Anthea Guthrie

BASILDON BOND CENTENARY GARDEN Designer: William Quarmby (Quarmby Landscaping & Design) Sponsor: Basildon Bond

A LITERARY GARDEN Designers: Martin Cook & Bonnie Davies

HAE-WOO-SO (EMPTYING ONE'S MIND) Designer: Jihae Hwang (Muun) Sponsors: Suncheon Bay Garden Expo 2013, Gwangju City (South Korea)

A POSTCARD FROM WALES Designers: Kati Crome & Maggie Hughes Sponsor: Trecor Investments

THE ART OF YORKSHIRE Designer: Gillespies

FEVER-TREE'S TREE HOUSE GARDEN Designer: Stephen Hall (Stephen Hall Design) Sponsor: Fever-Tree

GENERATION GARDENS

A FRUITFUL GARDEN Designer: Deakin Lock Garden Design Sponsors: John Woods Nurseries, The Sun Newspaper

MIRACLE-GRO'WERS LEARNING JOURNEY – FRUIT & VEGETABLES Designer: The Garden Design Centre Sponsor: The Scotts Miracle-Gro Company

MIRACLE-GRO'WERS LEARNING JOURNEY – FLOWERS Designer: Geoffrey Whiten Sponsor: The Scotts Miracle-Gro Company

LOOKING FORWARD WITH THE PAST Designer: Val Christman Sponsor: The Sun Newspaper

SHOW GARDENS 2012

LAND'S END: A RURAL MUSE Designer: Adam Frost Sponsor: Land's End Europe Ltd

A CELEBRATION OF CARAVANNING Designer: Jo Thompson Sponsor: The Caravan Club

THE WORLD VISION GARDEN Designer: FlemonsWarlandDesign Sponsor: World Vision

THE BREWIN DOLPHIN GARDEN Designer: Cleve West Sponsor: Brewin Dolphin

HOMEBASE TEENAGE CANCER TRUST GARDEN Designer: Joe Swift Sponsor: Homebase

THE ARTHRITIS RESEARCH UK GARDEN Designer: Thomas Hoblyn Sponsor: Arthritis Research UK

THE M&G GARDEN Designer: Andy Sturgeon Sponsor: M&G Investments

THE LAURENT-PERRIER BICENTENARY GARDEN Designer: Arne Maynard Sponsor: Champagne Laurent-Perrier

THE TELEGRAPH GARDEN Designer: Sarah Price Sponsor: The Daily Telegraph

THE RBC BLUE WATER GARDEN Designer: Prof Nigel Dunnett & The Landscape Agency Sponsor: Royal Bank of Canada

FURZEY GARDENS Designer: Chris Beardshow Ltd

THE L'OCCITANE IMMORTELLE GARDEN Designer: Peter Dowle Sponsor: L'Occitane en Provence

THE WESTLAND MAGICAL GARDEN Designer: Diarmuid

Gavin Sponsor: Westland Horticulture

TRAILFINDERS AUSTRALIAN GARDEN PRESENTED BY FLEMING'S Designer: Jason Hodges Sponsors: Trailfinders, Fleming's Nurseries

ROOFTOP WORKPLACE OF TOMORROW Designer: Patricia Fox (Aralia Garden Design) Sponsor: RBS in association with Walworth Garden Farm

QUIET TIME: DMZ FORBIDDEN GARDEN Designer: Jihae Hwang Sponsors: Muum, Korean Air, The Dowager Viscountess Rothermere, gardenlink

FRESH GARDENS

RAINBOWS CHILDREN'S HOSPICE GARDEN Designers: Chris Gutteridge, Ant Cox & Jon Owens (Second Nature Gardens)

THE QR CODE GARDEN Designer: Jade Goto in collaboration with Shelley Mosco of Green Graphite Ltd Sponsors: Scotscape Ltd, Treebox Ltd

THE SOFT MACHINE Designer: Tomaz Bavdez Sponsor: Humko Bled Ltd

PETRA – TRANQUILLITY SET IN STONE Designer: Benjamin Wincott Sponsor: Global Stone Paving

THE BRADSTONE PANACHE GARDEN Designer: Caroline E Butler Sponsor: Bradstone – sponsor of the Chris Beardshaw Mentoring Scholarship

OUT OF THE BLUE Designer: Alan Gardner Sponsors: Lindum, Alan Gardner

CLIMATE CALM GARDEN Designer: Nicholas Dexter Garden Designs Sponsors: Southern Water, Thames Water, South East Water, Sutton and East Surrey Water

GREEN WITH... Designer: Tony Smith Sponsor: Easigrass – The Artificial Grass Company

GLAMOURLANDS: A TECHNO-FOLLY Designers: Tony Heywood & Alison Condie represented by Vigo Gallery

THE RENAULT GARDEN Designer: James Basson Sponsor: Renault UK

ARTISAN GARDENS

PLANT EXPLORER'S GARDEN Designers: Karolina Tercjak & other SAC students Sponsor: Scottish Agricultural College

THE BRONTËS' YORKSHIRE GARDEN Designer: Tracy Foster Sponsor: Welcome to Yorkshire

PEPA'S STORY Designer: Borut Benedejcic Sponsors: Municipality Sežana, Municipality Komen, Municipality Hrpelje Kozina, Municipality Divača, Municipality Sgonico Zgonik

HERBERT SMITH GARDEN FOR WATERAID Designer: Patricia Thirion & Janet Honour (A Touch of France Garden Design) Sponsor: Herbert Smith

NATURALLY DRY – A WILLIAM WORDSWORTH-INSPIRED GARDEN Designer: Vicky Harris Sponsor: Veolia Water

THE APCO GARDEN Designers: Ruth Willmott & Frederic Whyte (Willmott Whyte) Sponsor: APCO Worldwide

THE PLANKBRIDGE SHEPHERD'S HUT GARDEN Designer: Woolcott & Smith Garden Design (Adam Woolcott & Jonathan Smith) Sponsor: Plankbridge Hutmakers

SATOYAMA LIFE Designer: Kazuyuki Ishihara Sponsors: Ishihara Kazuyuki Design Laboratory Co Lts., HB – 101, Cats Co Ltd, Sekisui Hime Tokai Co Ltd, Kubiki Co Ltd, Act, Jyutaro, Kazahana Tokyo Co Ltd

GENERATION GARDENS

THE COURTYARD GARDEN Designer: Geoff Whiten Sponsors: The Scotts Miracle-Gro Company, The Sun

MIRACLE-GRO'WERS LEARNING JOURNEY – FRUIT & VEGETABLES Designer: The Garden Design Centre Sponsor: The Scotts Miracle-Gro Company

MIRACLE-GRO'WERS LEARNING JOURNEY – FLOWER GARDEN Designer: Geoffry Whiten Sponsor: The Scotts Miracle-Gro Company

BEE UP FRONT GARDEN Designer: Val Christman Sponsor: The Sun

Please note: all gardens shown in 2010–2012 are listed above; whereas only gardens that are illustrated have been listed for years pre-2010.

INDEX

Figures in *italics* indicate captions

A
Aberconwy, 3rd Lord *10*
Acer palmatum 103
Achillea 71
　'Taygetea' *62*
acrylics 143
Agapanthus 58
Agave americana 69
　'Mediopicta Alba' *58*
Agrostemma githago 49
Albert, Prince 8
Alchemilla mollis 56, 62, 167
Allium 52, 53, 55, 71, 160
　A. atropurpureum 49
　A. cristophii 62
　A. nigrum 62
　A. stipitatum 'Mount Everest' *49*
alpine strawberries 155
aluminium 135
Anethum graveolens (dill) 185
annual chrysanthemums 68
Anthriscus sylvestris 'Ravenswing' *56, 71*
Aponogeton distachyos 110
apple trees *181*
Aquilega 53
　'Black Barlow' *53*
Arabic gardens *18*, 18, 22
arches 28
　woven hazel *45*
Armeria 167
　A. maritima (sea thrift) *149*
Arrowsmith, Chris 172, *173*
Artemisia 56
　A. dracunculus 179
　A. ludoviciana 62
'Artisan' gardens 13
artworks 202–17
　integrated approach to 210
　personalising space 214
　see also sculptures
Asarum eurpaeum 79
Ask Design Management 172, 173
Astelia chathamica 54
astrantias *79*
awnings 99

B
B & Q garden 76–7
Balston, Michael 11
bamboos *41*, 126–7
Banks, Sir Joseph 8
Barnett, Marcus *35*, 213
bay 74
Beaminster District Gardens and Allotment Society 11
beans *183*
bearded irises 53, *54, 56, 67*
　'Dutch Chocolate' *71*
　orange *47*
beehives *160*
bees *155*, 160
benches *84*, 88, 88–9, *89, 103*
　curved *149*
bikes *99*
biodiversity 154–5, *163*, 164, 170
birches (*Betula*) *61, 173, 190*
bird feeders *160*
bird's foot trefoil (*Lotus conriculatus*) 155

'black' ponds 106, *113*
Blom, Jinny 28, 46, 47
boats *17, 21*
borrowed landscapes 48, *49*
boundaries 28, *28*
box (*Buxus*) *56, 61*
　balls 22, *55, 67, 129*
　cloud pruning 73
　in containers *79*
　hedging 22, 29, 54, *82*, 118
Bradley-Hole, Christopher 11
Brewin Dolphin garden 48–9
bricks 28
　brick paths *38, 39, 43*
Brockbank, Jane *163*
bronze fennel *181*
Brookes, John 190
Brundtland Commission 154
buildings 28, 82, 96–9
　green roofs *97, 148*, 155, *166, 166, 172, 172, 186*
　huts *85, 96*
　summerhouses 82, 96, *97*
Bupa Garden 64–5

C
cacti *147*
Calendula 72
camomile *38*
Cancer Research UK Garden 148–51, 200–1
canopies *95*
caravans *6*
cardoons *151, 181*
case studies
　B & Q garden 76–7
　Brewin Dolphin garden 48–9
　Cancer Research UK Garden 148–51, 200–1
　Daily Telegraph Garden *41*, 126–7
　Eco Chic 102–3
　Future Nature 172–3
　Laurent–Perrier Garden *25*, 46–7, 78–9
　M & G Garden 128–9, 216–17
　Monaco garden 100–1
　Summer Solstice 186–7
Centranthus rubber
　'Alba' *148*
　'Coccineaus' *148*
Cercidiphyllum japonicum 217
chairs *84, 85, 87*
chamomile *139*
Chelsea pensioners *14, 113*
Chetwood, Laurie 77
children 177
chives *181*
chrysanthemums 68
Cirsium rivulare 'Atropurpureum' *155*
citrus plants, pot-grown 184
classic gardens 21
clematis 160
climate change 58, 156
cloud pruning 73, *79*
coastal gardens 148–51
Collins, Patrick 77
colour
　coloured lighting *191*
　colour-themed planting *62*, 62–5, *65*
　materials 140–1

and sustainable gardens 164
composting 164
concrete *128*, 157
Conran, Sir Terence 199
containers 29, 72–5
　anchoring 215
　black planters *147*
　colours 140, *141*
　growing produce in 184–5
　growing vegetables in *179*
　metal planters *135, 181*
Convolvulus cneorum 74
copper pools *159*
Cordyline 58
　C. australis 149
corncockle *49*
corn poppy (*Papaver rhoeas*) *56*
Cornus controversa 151
cottage gardens 52, 56–7
cow parsley (*Anthriscus*) *56*
cowslip (*Primula veris*) 155
Craddock, Tony 193, 195
Cubero, David *115*
cupboards, outdoor *99*
Cycas revoluta 58

D
daffodils 52–3
dahlias 53
Daily Telegraph Garden *41*, 126–7
Davidson, Charlie 85
Davies, Iestyn *117*
decking *28*, 28, *38, 91*, 91, *95*
　with chamomile *139*
　laying 91
　with steel mesh *139*
　types of 91
del Buono, Tommaso 186, 187
Dexter, Nicholas *137*
Dianthus 155
　D. carthusianorum 69
Digitalis (foxgloves) *54, 71, 160*
dill (*Anethum graveolens*) 185
dog kennel 22
doors 28
dovecotes *99*
drainpipes *172*
drought-tolerant planting 58–9, 69
Dunnett, Nigel 155, *169*, 173

E
Eberle, Sarah 28, 100, *101*
Echeveria 58, 74
Eco Chic 102–3
edging water *113*
　stone edging *128*
electricians 195
Elizabeth II, Queen *10*
entrances 28, 44–5
Erodium manescavii 69
Ewing, Andrew *113*, 118–19

F
fairy lights *99*
Fan, Shao 21
fencing 28, *36*, 36, 142
　rustic *44*
fennel 62
　bronze *181*
ferns 155
Festival of Britain 9

Festuca gautieri 66
fig trees *184*
fire pits 133
fireplace, outdoor *187*
Fleming's Nurseries of Australia 83
Foeniculum vulgare 'Purpurem' *62*
formal gardens *22*, 22
　planting schemes for 60–1
foxgloves (*Digitalis*) *54, 71, 160*
Fox, Patricia 145
French tarragon (*Artemisia dracunculus*) 179
'Fresh' gardens 13
front gardens *36*, 157
Frost, Adam 30
furniture 133
　chairs *84, 85, 87*
　Monaco garden *101*
Future Nature 172–3

G
gabions 134, *135, 141, 147*
gates 28, *45*
　moon gates *45*, 46, *47*
Gaura lindheimeri 69
Gavin, Dairmuid 11, *14*, 28, 199
Gazerwitz, Paul 186, *187*
geraniums
　G. phaeum 'Album' *71*
　G. sylvaticum 'Mayflower' *47*
Geum 62
Giubbilei, Luciano 25
glass 29, 132
　coloured
　　panes *141*
　　sculptures *207*
　pebbles *118*
　recycled *165*
　screens *37*
　sculptures *117, 125*
　tiles *195*
　using in the garden 143
Gould, Kate 102, *103*
grasses *47, 53, 55*
　Stipa 47, 53, 54
grass paths *142, 187*
Great Pavilion *12*, 52
greenhouses 82
green roofs *97, 148*, 155, *166, 166, 172, 172, 186*
Guinness, Bunny 99
Gunnera manicata 127

H
Halifax Garden `These Four Walls' *123*
Hallam, Adrian 172, 173
Hall, Marney 22
halogen lighting *193*, 193
Harber, David 208
hedges 29, 142
　box 22, 29, 54, *82*, 118
　Brewin Dolphin garden 48, *49*
　hornbeam 29, *47*
　tiered *25*
　yew *126*, 150, *150*
herbs *77, 176*, 177
　growing in raised beds *181*
　herb 'wheel' *179*
　how to grow 179
Heuchera

'Peach Flambé' 62
purple-leaved 167
Hill, Sue and Peter 22
history of the RHS Chelsea Flower
Show 8–11
holly (*Ilex crenata*) 217
hornbeam hedging 29, 47
horse's head sculpture 207
Horticultural Society of London 8
hostas 79
Howarth, Maggy 125
huts
beach huts 96
'rib-cage' timber 85

I
Ilex crenata (holly) 217
industrial mesh 28
insect hotels 76, 77, 165
Iris
'Action Front' 41
wetland 71
white 54
see also bearded irises
iron railings 28, 36, 44
ivy (*Hedera*) 32

J
Japanese gardening 73
judging panels 12
juniper 61
Jurassic malt limestone 217

keyhole sculpture 207
kitchens, outdoor 82, 83

L
Laurent–Perrier Garden 25, 46–7,
78–9
lavender (*Lavandula*) 56
L. angustifolia 77
lawns 48
layered planting 63
LED lighting 193, 193
lemon balm 181
Lennox-Boyd, Arabella 126, 127
Lenti, Paola 151
lettuce 181, 183, 184
Libertia grandiflora 74
lighting 188–201
case studies 200–1
choosing 200
coloured 191
employing an electrician 195
ground-level highlights 194
illuminating effects 192–3
illuminating water 196–7
and outdoor living 190
photovoltaic 190
primary light sources 193
specific objects 190, 191, 194–5
techniques 196–7
and water features 117, 119
limestone
Jurassic malt 217
paths 150
slabs 31
Limonium platyphyllum 69
Linnaeus, Carl 21, 142
living walls 103, 166, 167, 172
loggia, timber 129

logs
log cuts 31
stacked 159

M
M&G Garden 128–9, 216–17
McVicar, Jekka 179, 185
magical and mad gardens 22, 22
Main Avenue 6
materials 28, 28, 29, 130–51
acrylics 143
artworks 205, 205
case studies 148–51
colours 140–1
concrete 128, 157
containers 72
entrances 44, 45
gabions 134, 135, 141, 147
paths 38, 38, 43
Perspex 29, 132
and plant choice 54
steps 31
thinking outside the box 146–7
water features 125, 126
Witan Wisdom Garden 137
see also glass; metal; recycled
materials; stone; timber
Matthiola incana 67
May, James 11
Meconopsis poppies 53
Mediterranean gardens 18, 18, 22
mesh 28, 31, 85, 139
metal 132, 134–5, 147
aluminium 135
artworks 205
gabions 134, 135, 141, 147
planters 135, 181
steel 132, 134, 135
decking with steel mesh
139
screens 142
sculptures 208
water features 125
zinc tanks 147
minimalist gardens 17–18
planting schemes 66–7
mirrors 126, 204
misting machines 117
mixed-style gardens 17
Monaco garden 100–1
moon gates 45, 46, 47
Morus alba 'Platanifolia' (mulberry)
76, 77
mosaic paths 141
moss tracks 32
mulberry (*Morus alba* 'Platanifolia')
76, 77
mustard (*Brassica juncea*) 185
Myers, Robert 148, 149, 200, 201

N
Nash, Philip 209, 215
naturalistic-style planting 70–1
Nature Ascending 163
Nepata 56
Nixon, Philip 35
Nordfjell, Ulf 21
nursery displays 6
Nymphaea alba (waterlily) 126, 127

oak sculpture 151

Oceanico Garden 199
Oda, Mari-Ruth 94
Oenothera macrocarpa 69
office, outdoor 145
Osteospermum 74
outdoor living 80–103
case studies 100–3
offices 145
pavilions 86–7
shade and structure 94–5
see also buildings; lighting;
seating

P
Papaver rhoeas (corn poppy) 56
Parrotia persica 70, 205
parties 99
paths 28, 29, 38–43
artwork 214
brick 38, 39, 43
grass 142, 187
lighting 197, 197
mosaic 141
Portuguese limestone 150
in productive gardens 187
slate 126, 127
pavilions 86–7
Cancer Research UK Garden 151
paving 28, 47
linear 39
permeable 103
and water management 155
peony (*Paeonia*) 201
pergolas 43, 82, 201
Perry, Stuart 123
Perspex 29, 132, 143
orange screens 142
pest control 164
Phatanus x *hispanica* 127
Phlomis russeliana 69
photovoltaic lighting 190
Phyllostachys bamboo 127
Pinus sylvestris 'Watereri' 61
planters *see* containers
planting 50–79
case studies 76–9
colours and textures 52
colour-themed 62, 62–5, 65
containers 72–5
cottage-garden 52, 56–7
drought-tolerant 58–9, 69
formal 60–1
layered 63
living walls 167
M & G Garden 216
minimalist 66–7
modern schemes 54–5
Monaco garden 101
naturalistic 70–1
paths 39
sustainable gardens 157, 173
for wildlife 68–9
plastics 29
plastic bottles 171
Platts, Roger 128, 129
ponds 113
'black' 106, 113
edging 113
fish in 128
and wildlife 160
pools

circular 128
copper 159
formal 22
self-contained 107
and sustainable gardens 157,
172, 173
swimming pools 86–7, 101–2
poppies (*Meconopsis*) 53
Portuguese limestone paths 150
Primula veris (cowslip) 155
productive gardens 174–87
case studies 186–7
growing your own (GYO) 176–9
maximising use of space 183
raised beds 170, 171, 179, 180,
181
Provence-style garden 31
pruning
cloud pruning 73, 79
Pterocarya fraxinifolia 127

R
raised beds
growing vegetables and herbs in
170, 171, 179, 180, 181, 187
rammed earth walls 32, 43
Randall-Page, Peter 204
RBC New Wild Garden 169
recycled materials 29, 154, 155, 158–
9, 170
'bridges' using recycled timber
149
glass 165
'greenhouse' made from 171
roofing tiles 159
tables made from 147, 171
terracotta pots 159
white goods 159
recycling water 159
reflections in water 106, 118–19, 126
rills 106, 107, 172, 172
Rock Bank 11
rocket (*Eruca vericaria*) 185
rocks
in water features 127
rodgersias 79
romantic gardens 17, 17
roofing tiles 159
Rooftop Workplace of Tomorrow 145
rope-houses 160
rosemary 181
roses (*Rosa*) 36
'Burgundy Ice' 77
'Reine des Violettes' 14
Royal Family 10
rural gardens 154

S
salad crops
growing in containers 185
Salvia (sage) 52, 71, 167, 181
Salvia officinalis 179
sandstone slabs 39
Sarracenia 113
Savills Garden 34–5, 35
savory (*Satureja montana*) 179
scaffold boards and poles 102
Scarpa, Carlo 46
Schinus molle 61
screens 28, 29, 36, 36, 142
orange Perspex 142

steel 142
  white 37, 94
sculptures 6, 150
  anchoring 215
  case study 216–17
  ceramic 94
  circular 46, 47
  'energy wave' 217
  glass 117, 125
  large 205
  lighting 190, 194
  living 22
  locating 206–9, 207, 216
  oak 151
  personalising space 214, 214,
    215
  pineapple cones 211
  positioning 209
  stone 205
  and trees 207
  wall sculptures 48, 48, 49
  and water features 109, 110
sea thrift (*Armeria maritima*) 149
seating 82, 84–93
  benches 84, 88, 88–9, 89, 103,
    149
  Cancer Research UK Garden 148
  chairs 84, 85, 87
  cubed 82
  lighting seating areas 192, 197,
    200
  outdoor sofas 83, 90–1, 91, 93
  wood block 39
Sedum
  on green roofs 155, 166
  matting 58
  S. telephium 'Purple emperor' 69
Sempervivum 53, 58, 74
setts 28, 43, 79
shade, planting for 77
sheds 82
Sheffield University 172
  BUGS project 154–5
show gardens 12–13, 13–14
  artwork in 204, 210
  planting 52
  and sustainability 154
slabs
  limestone 31
  sandstone 39
slate paths 126, 127
sodium lighting 193
sofas, outdoor 83, 90–1, 91, 93
soil conservation 164
Soleirolia soleirolii 61
spatial division 17
sponsors 15
Stachys 69
  S. byzantina 52, 69, 71
stainless steel panels 102
steel 132, 134, 135
  decking with steel mesh 139
  screens 142
  sculptures 208
  water features 125, 135
steps 28, 30–1
  designing 30–1
Stipa
  S. gigantea 47, 53, 54
  S. tenuissima 47, 67, 69
stocks 67

stone 28, 132
  edging 128
  paths 39, 43
  plinths 85
  sculptures 205
  steps 31
  water features 110
Stone, Paul 170, 171
stories, gardens telling 21, 21
strawberries
  alpine 155
Stuart-Smith, Tom 22, 53, 63, 73
Sturgeon, Andy 15, 41, 91, 143
  Cancer Research UK Garden
    150–1
  M&G Garden 128–9, 216–17
summerhouses 82, 95, 96
Summer Solstice 186–7
sustainability 152–73
  and artwork 211
  and biodiversity 154–5, 163,
    164, 170
  case study 172–3
  and garden planning 156–7
  green roofs 97, 148, 155, 166,
    166, 172, 172, 186
  ideas for 170
  living walls 103, 166, 167, 172
  Nature Ascending 163
  places of change 170–1
  planting combinations 157
  RBC New Wild Garden 169
  statements with 164–5
  sustainable development 154
  water management 155, 156
  and wildlife 155, 159, 160–1
  see also recycled materials
sweet Williams 56
Swift, Joe 14
swimming pools 86–7, 101–2

T
tables
  made from recycled materials
    147, 171
tamarisk (*Tamarix gallica*) 149
terracotta pots 159
Thompson, Angus 163
thyme (*Thymus vulgaris*) 155, 179, 181
Tillia europaea 'Pallida' 76
timber 132, 132, 138–9
  advantages of 138
  benches 88, 89
  fencing 36
  loggia 129
  oak 139
  offcuts 132
  painted poles 171
  pallets 159
  pergolas 43
  recycled 149
  'rib-cage' huts 85
  walls 139
  Western red cedar 139
Times Eureka Garden 213
tomatoes 183
topiary 48, 49
Tourism Malaysian Garden 115
Trachycarpus fortunei palms 61
trade stands 12, 13
Trailfinders Australian Garden 87

trees 52, 52, 53
  Acer palmatum 103
  apple 181
  birch (*Betula*) 61, 173, 190
  borrowed landscapes 48, 49
  columnar oak 47
  fig trees 184
  juniper 61
  Laurent-Perrier garden 78, 79
  and lighting 190
  mulberry 76
  Parrotia persica 70, 205
  Phatanus x *hispanica* 127
  Pinus sylvestris 'Watereri' 61
  pleached limes 76
  Pterocarya fraxinifolia 127
  Schinus molle 61
  and sculptures 207
  Trachycarpus fortuneii 61
  and water features 128
trelliswork 28
tulips 155

U
ultraviolet acrylics 143
umbellifer 56
urban gardens 100
  sustainable 154, 164

V
valerian 148
vegetables 176–87
  in containers 184–5
  growing in raised beds 170, 171,
    179, 180, 181, 187
  and sustainability 165, 170
Verbascum 58, 67
  V. bombyciferum 'Polar Summer'
    148
  V. phoeniceum 69
Viburnum
  opulus 'Roseum' 54
  V. rhytidophyllum 52
vines 68

W
walkways 28, 38
walls 28, 29, 32–5, 35, 142
  and artwork 211
  form and texture 33
  ivy climbing on 32
  living 103, 166, 167, 172
  moss tracks on 32
  and productive gardens 183
  rammed earth 32, 43
  scaffold boards and poles 102
  and stacked logs 159
  timber 139
  wall sculptures 48, 48, 49
  and water features 117, 120
water 104–29
  artworks 205
  case studies 126–9
  channelling 125
  and green roofs 166
  illuminating 196–7
  making it work 106–7
  management of 155, 156
  moving 107, 116–25, 128
  recycling 159
  reflections in 106, 118–19, 126

still 108–15, 128, 129
  and wildlife 113, 128, 163
water butts 56
water features 28, 106, 128
  arcs 125
  'black' ponds 106, 113
  chutes 125
  drops of water 120, 125
  edging 113
  Halifax Garden 'These Four
    Walls' 123
  jets for vertical foam 118
  Laurent-Perrier garden 78, 79
  'plug hole' 93
  rills 106, 107, 172, 173
  rocks in 127
  sculptures 29
  shape of 128
  steel 125, 135
  swirling vortex 117
  tables 91
  waterfalls 117
  see also ponds; pools
water hawthorn 110
watering cans 56
waterlily (*Nymphaea alba*) 126, 127
Wedgwood, John 8
West, Cleve
  Brewin Dolphin garden 48–9
  Bupa Garden 64–5
Western red cedar 139
wheat 68
white goods, recycled 159
wild flowers 68
wildlife
  bees 155, 160
  Future Nature garden 172
  insect hotels 76, 77, 165
  and lighting 190
  planting for 68–9
  and sustainability 155, 159
    attracting wildlife 160–1
  and water 113, 128, 163
wildlife gardens 21, 21–2
Witan Wisdom Garden 137
Wong, James 115
wood *see* timber

Y
Yarrow, Heather 22
yew
  cloud pruning 73
  hedges 126, 150, 150
  topiary 48, 49
York stone 28

Z
Zantedeschia 62
zinc tanks 147

ACKNOWLEDGEMENTS

In October 2009, for the first edition of this book, I wrote:-

'At the heart of this book is an immense gratitude to all those people who have created, and continue to create, gardens at the RHS Chelsea Flower Show. This book focuses primarily on the show from 2004 to 2009, but such recognition and thanks span the show's history. Without the vision, skill, enthusiasm and energy of the exhibitors – plus the seemless organisation by the RHS shows department – the RHS Chelsea Flower Show wouldn't be able to lead the way in garden design and plantsmanship.

Garden designers, landscape architects, nurserymen, landscape contractors, lighting engineers, sculptors, water specialists, educational establishments...the list of people involved is endless. Yet by coming together in the name of gardens and horticulture, their collective skills inspire and inform thousands of us each year. It may seem obvious, but without them this book really wouldn't be possible.'

And so it continues to be true. This book, which now spans the show from 2004 to 2012, is a celebration of all things Chelsea, and in a way, all things garden. It reflects taste, attitudes and ideas, many of which eventually filter down to our domestic spaces. I, like so many people, love the show, and now in its 100th year, it is an extra special time to celebrate. Long may it continue.

Together, I hope we have made a book that continues to keep the spirit of Chelsea alive, helping home gardeners to get the most out of their private space.

Chris Young, Ketton, Rutland
July 2012

PHOTOGRAPHY CREDITS

All photographs are by Steven Wooster with the exception of the following.

(t) top (b) bottom, (c) centre, (l) left, (r) right

ALAMY Andrea Jones Images 40-41, 42 (b), 76-77, 159 (t); Ben Pipe Photography 141 (l); Jo Whitworth 69 (tl); Mark Bolton 73 (bl); Martin Hughes-Jones 21, 145 (b); Miriam Heppell 48-9; Neil Hepworth 118 (tr); Rob Whitworth Garden Photography 63 (l)
CLIVE NICHOLS 195 (b)
CORBIS Mark Bolton 6 (tl), Reuters 7 (br)
GAP PHOTOS Anne Green-Armytage 15; Clive Nichols 138 (b), 159 (br); Elke Borkowski/design Fritz Doepper 196 (b); Friedrich Strauss 99 (c & r); Heather Edwards 69 (tr); J S Sira 18 (t); Jo Whitworth 12; John Glover 23; Linda Burgess 91 (b); Marcus Harpur 20, 45 (t, r); 63 (r), 193 (br); Mark Bolton 154 (t), 160 (b), 174 (c); Martin Hughes-Jones 21; Michael Howes 24; Michael King 91 (r); Rob Whitworth 17, 119 (t), 179 (r) (design: Jon Wheatley, Mary Payne and Terry Porter); Sabina Ruber 16; Zara Napier 73 (tr); Steven Studd 145 (t) Steven Wooster; 209 (l)
GARDEN COLLECTION Andrew Lawson 23; 31 (tr); 70, 72 (r), 86-7, 91 (t), 106 (t and b); 148-9; 168-9; 184 (l); 196 (tr); 200-201; Derek Harris 100-1, 114-5; Derek St Romaine 7 (l & tr); 12 (t); 37 (t); Liz Eddison 13 b, 14 a, 18 b, 38 bl, 42 a, 53 br; 55 l, 89 a, 98 br; Neil Sutherland 128-9; Torie Chugg 33 c, 89 b, 95 a, 112 inset, 113 cr

GARDEN EXPOSURES ANDREA JONES 22
GARDEN WORLD IMAGES Andrea Jones 14(b), 144, 216 (b), 217
GETTY IMAGES Adam Stevens 85 (t); Ben Pipe Photography 171, 207 (br); Chris Jackson 212-13; Ming Tang-Evans 119 (b), 133 (t), 177 (tr), 184 (r); Photolibrary/Garden Picture Library/Andrea Jones 73 (br); /David Dixon 31 (b); /Hemant Jariwala 113 (b); /Mel Watson 69 (br); /Michael Howes 185 (r); /Ron Evans 69 (bc); Rosalind Simon 205 (l); Sarah Cuttle 125 (l)
HARPUR GARDEN IMAGES Jerry Harpur 2, 4, 43 (r); Marcus Harpur 34, 116 (br), 120 (tl), 122, 130 (tl), 209 (r), 215 (br)
MARIANNE MAJERUS GARDEN IMAGES Andrew Lawson 19, Marianne Majerus 97 (tl), 108, 186
OCTOPUS PUBLISHING GROUP David Sarton 39 (tl), (bl) and (br), 50 (t), 51 (b), 54 (br), 55 (r), 56 (tl & b), 57 (b), 58, 59 (br), 62 (c), 66, 67 (b), 71 (tr), 74 (tl), 85 (b), 118 (tl), 124 (br), 130 (bl), 133 (br), 135 (bl), 154 (t), 166 (tr), 174 (tl & bl), 175 (tl), 180 (l &r), 182 (bl), 183 (r), 185 (l)
PHOTOSHOT Red Cover/Hugh Palmer 118 (c)
PRESS ASSOCIATION IMAGES PA Wire 11
ROYAL HORTICULTURAL SOCIETY Lindley Library 9 (t & b), all 10; Neil Hepworth 6 (bl)